A DANGEROUS

JOURNEY

Those Who Become Jesus' Disciples

Reginald F. Davis

To: Henrietta Palmer
Stay on the Journey

Reginald F. Davis

3/2/17

i

A DANGEROUS JOURNEY

Those Who Become Jesus' Disciples

Reginald F. Davis

Christian Publishing House
Cambridge, Ohio

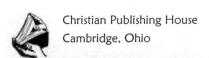

Unless otherwise stated, Scripture quotations are from *The Holy Bible, Updated American Standard Version (UASV)®*, Copyright © 2016 by Christian Publishing House, Professional Conservative Christian Publishing of the Good News!

A DANGEROUS JOURNEY: Those Who Become Jesus' Disciples

ISBN-10: 1-945757-36-1

ISBN-13: 978-1-945757-36-5

Acknowledgements

I would like to acknowledge the support of my family, i.e. my wife Myrlene who encouraged me to continue the research and the prayers of my three children Isaac, Nandi, and Joel. Also, I want to thank the whole Davis family and friends for their prayers and encouragement. They are too numerous to name. Last, I want to thank Edward Andrews and the Christian Publishing House team for accepting this work for publication. Their input and suggestions have been invaluable.

To contact Reginald F. Davis for speaking engagements, lectures, and preaching opportunities please contact the following:

drreginalddavis1964@gmail.com

(757) 719-7270 cell

Table of Contents

Acknowledgements iv

Introduction.. 1

CHAPTER ONE Jesus the Inconvenient Leader 21

CHAPTER TWO Expect Temptation..................... 45

CHAPTER THREE Expect Rejection 55

CHAPTER FOUR Expect Criticism 66

CHAPTER FIVE Expect Loneliness....................... 76

CHAPTER SIX Expect Betrayal............................. 85

CHAPTER SEVEN Expect Persecution 94

CHAPTER EIGHT Expect Death........................... 110

CHAPTER NINE The Great Reward................... 122

CHAPTER TEN The Conclusion 136

Bibliography... 148

Introduction

> Suffering, failure, loneliness, sorrow, discouragement, and death will be part of your journey, but the Kingdom of God will conquer all these horrors. No evil can resist grace forever.—Brennan Manning

We are living in some very dangerous times; times of whih human relations are deteriorating; families are falling apart; communities are in a crisis, gun violence is an everyday occurrence, the government is divided, and the faith and witness of many Christians are recoiling into a private affair because of the risk of persecution. Society has become so narcissistic many people don't want to hear the truth of the gospel of Jesus Christ. The time is upon us of which "For there will be a time when they will not put up with sound teaching, but in accordance with their own desires, they will accumulate teachers for themselves to have their ears tickled."[1] (2 Timothy 4:3) There are people in society who will try to harm and persecute Christians for disagreeing with a culture that does not acknowledge nor honor God. They do not believe in the Lordship of Jesus Christ. In America and other parts of the world Christians are being killed for their faith in Jesus Christ. To stand for Christian principles could mean death as was demonstrated in Charleston, South Carolina, Roseburg, Oregon, and other places. Without hyperbole or exaggeration, the speed of attacks is accelerating against Christians, and we must prepare ourselves for more attacks here in America. It is a sad commentary that in such a hostile culture where followers of Jesus Christ are facing more and more opposition to their faith, there are enemies not only outside the walls of the church but inside as well. The church (ecclesia) of which Jesus Christ founded is under attack from without and from within. Many pastors who are

---

[1] Or *to tell them what they want to hear*

preaching the uncompromising gospel of Jesus Christ are under attack. Some are voted out of the pulpit; others are leaving the church due to conflict, and some around the world are being killed. Christian ministry is becoming so much more challenging, stressful, and abusive that many pastors are opting to get out than staying in. The persecution and abuse within and without the church have become so riveting; many Christian leaders are leaving at an alarming rate.

The reason attacks are happening within the church is too many Christians are fearful of standing against wrong, evil, and injustice. They are cultural Christians who live as if the church is a social club, a fraternity or sorority. Forget what is right, and just before God, many Christians have made their fellowship with social clubs more important than their discipleship with Jesus Christ. They live their lives by their own righteousness but will not submit to the righteousness of God (Roman 10:3). "Their conduct is not measured against the standard set by the gospel. They have developed their own philosophies, which they attempt to pawn off as Christian faith. The big problem in these cases is the fact that these men and women have arrived at their conclusions apart from any study of the Bible. The Bible sits dusty on the shelf. These people are biblically illiterate. Their knowledge of the Bible is that of a child."[2] This is the reason, so few Christians become disciples; they do not commit to the study of the Word of God. They don't make time to be under the teaching of the Word. Many say they are too busy. Busyness has become a weapon against their discipleship, which is a trick of the enemy. The more the enemy can keep Christians busy, the more he can cheat them out of their discipleship of which they will have no power to know how to resist an ungodly culture and how to be effective for the Kingdom of God. There is no way the twelve disciples of Jesus could have

---

[2] William Wilberforce, Real Christianity, Regal Books, 2006, 21-22.

carried on his message and known how to lead a Christian movement in such a hostile culture had they not subjected themselves under the teaching of Jesus. So, if people are going to follow Jesus, they must commit themselves to the teaching of Jesus. They must commit to Bible Study and prayer meetings that are critical for their training. If they refuse the training, they cannot be disciples. They can only be fans, not disciples.

Not only are many Christians biblically illiterate, but they also have never been born again by the power of the Holy Spirit. They may have confessed but have not possessed Christ. Many were never brought up with standards and spiritual values to pass on to their children and grandchildren. They rely on their secular knowledge to guide them on a spiritual journey. Therefore, they are in rebellion against God and the Lordship of Jesus Christ because "The natural man does not accept the things of the Spirit of God, for they are foolishness to him, and he is not able to understand them because they are examined spiritually."[3] (1 Corinthians 2:14) Due to their functioning without the Holy Spirit, they form click groups within the church to get their way, and when they cannot get their way they launch attacks within as the world attacks without. These so-called Christians align themselves with people of the world to undermine the influence of the Christian church and its leadership. But, this phenomenon of persecution and abuse is not new. When Jesus Christ first established the early church, he said, "The gates of Hades (i.e., Hell)[4] will not overpower it." (Matthew

---

[3] CPH: Recommended Reading: EXPLAINING THE HOLY SPIRIT: Basic Bible Doctrines of the Christian Faith by Edward D. Andrews

http://www.christianpublishers.org/apps/webstore/products/show/6565103

[4] Hades is the standard transliteration into English of the corresponding Greek word haides, which occurs ten times in the UASV. (Matt. 11:23; 16:18; Lu 10:15; 16:23; Ac 2:27, 31; Rev. 1:18; 6:8; 20:13,

16:18) Jesus never said or suggested that the church would not be attacked, undermined, and persecuted. Over the centuries, God's people have been stoned, sawn asunder, slain by the sword, thrown to hungry lions, destitute, ill-treated, etc. but the church is still here. Jesus assured the church that suffering, persecution, ill-treatment, and tragedy after tragedy wouldn't have victory over the church. Christians all over the world must understand that we are truly in a spiritual warfare. William Wilberforce said, "We will have a degree of struggle that will require discipline and tough obedience till the end. Remember, we are at war. We battle a culture that is out of tune with God, a personality shaped outside the influence of the Holy Spirit, and an unseen universe in which powerful evil forces are allowed to exercise a degree of autonomy until Jesus Christ returns.[5]

Jesus Christ our Savior and Commander in Chief wants us to follow him. Jesus never commanded us to worship him. He always pointed to His Father. Too often Christians worship him as a way to escape following him. Harry Emerson Fosdick hits the nail on the head:

You see what we have done with Christ—we have kept his name on the label, but we have changed the contents of the bottle. That is a summary of much of Christendom's history—the name kept on the label "Christ," but the contents not of his moral quality. We cannot suppose—can we?—that that suddenly has stopped in our time? Upon the contrary, the churches of this country are full of people who worship Christ, who have no idea what Christ means about war, race, relationships, the color

---

14.) It has the underlying meaning of 'a place of the dead, where they are conscious of nothing, awaiting a resurrection, for both the righteous and the unrighteous.' (John 5:28-29; Acts 24:15) It corresponds to "Sheol" in the OT.

[5] Ibid., 181-182.

line, about the money standards of the day, the profit motive in industry, than Constantine had about Christ's attitude toward his bloody imperialism, or the Duke of Avla about Christ's care for the victims of his persecution. This seems to me the very nub of the Christian problem today. . . . A Christianity that worships Christ emotionally but does not follow him morally is a convention sham, and too much of our ecclesiastical Christianity today is precisely that. Let us say it to ourselves in our beautiful churches, amid the loveliness of our architecture, lest we should ever be tempted to substitute esthetics for ethics or formal worship for downright righteousness. Jesus would care more about our attitude towards the color line or war than he would care about our processionals, however stately, and all our architecture, however fine. For obviously, Jesus, above all else, intended to be taken in earnest morally. Consider how easy it is to dispose of Christ by worshipping him, because we can thereby substitute theological opinion for spiritual experience.[6]

Therefore, to follow Christ is to reproduce him in our lives, actions, and struggle. Admiration of Christ must produce imitation of Him in the world. Those who are enlisting to follow Jesus Christ must be reminded of what this journey entails. This is a dangerous journey! Study the early Christians. Look at the life of Peter, Paul, Timothy, and those who imitated Christ. The journey was not easy, comfortable nor about compromising with the world. Years ago a prominent pastor named Sandy F. Ray calls the Christian journey a jungle. He said, "The jungle has shifted from the forest to the front office. The jungle is no longer crude,

---

[6] Harry Emerson Fosdick, Answers To Real Problems: Harry Emerson Fosdick Speaks To Our Time, Edited by Mark E. Yurs, Wipf and Stock Publishers, 2008, 31.

primitive, stupid, simple, and rude; the jungle has become sophisticated, clever, and suave. The beast is not hiding in a dark dungeon to pounce upon its victims. He is bold, brazen, and daring. This jungle is created by human behavior. . . .It is extremely attractive with glaring lights and fascinating entertainment. . . Pimps and prostitutes walk our streets brazenly, daring, and defiantly without shame or fear. Narcotics has become a most unholy, unhealthy, and death-peddling industry. It is crippling and slaying the youth of the nation, physically, morally, and spiritually."[7] Christians must understand that on this journey they are really "sheep among wolves."

To get to the destination of eternal life on this journey Jesus says, "Follow Me." This is a direct invitational command to become a disciple and leave behind everything we are attached to and join Jesus on a rough, tough, and dangerous journey that leads to defeat and then to victory, to death and then to life, to losing to ultimately winning. The Danish theologian Soren Kierkegaard said, "Now it is well enough known that Christ constantly uses the expression 'follower'; He never says anything about wanting admirers, admiring worshippers, adherents; and when he uses the expression 'disciple', He always so explains it that we can perceive that followers are meant, that they are not adherents of a doctrine but followers of a life, a life which had no adventitious marks of loftiness which would make it presumptuous on our part, or mere madness, to wish to resemble it."[8] We are called to discipleship not membership. There is a qualitative difference between membership and discipleship. Membership hears the clarion call of the Master but disciples follow and obey. Membership doesn't abide in

---

[7] Sandy F. Ray, Journeying Through A Jungle, BroadMan Press, 1979, 25-26.

[8] Soren Kierkegaard, Training In Christianity, Translated, With An Introduction And Notes, By Walter Lowrie, Princeton University Press, 1972, 231.

the Word of God but disciples cannot live without the Word of God. Membership lives according to the natural senses, but disciples live according to the Holy Spirit. In short, Jesus called disciples not members nor admirers to follow him. Admirers are not willing to obey and die in order to live in Christ; only disciples are.

Jesus made it clear that He is calling for disciples. This means disciples are called to sacrifice in order to gain, bear a cross in order to wear a crown, and enter into spiritual warfare in order to share in the victory with Jesus Christ. You may ask, "Why is this journey dangerous?" It is dangerous because the Kingdom of this world and the Kingdom of God are in conflict. Jesus started his campaign ministry to usher in the Kingdom of God against the Kingdom of this world. Jesus Christ came to "to proclaim good news[9] to the poor. He has sent me to proclaim release to the captives and recovering of sight to the blind, to set free those who are oppressed." (Luke 4:18) Jesus whole campaign ministry was about liberating the human condition and destroying the campaign of the prince of this world, of which violence, oppression, greed, injustice, and inequality are its normal operating principals. Jesus called disciples to join him in his campaign ministry to show the world that there is a better way and a much nobler path than the path of sin, evil, and injustice. Jesus made it clear that his campaign ministry is about loving people, serving people, delivering people, lifting up people, and saving people. It is a campaign ministry of "whosoever will" that includes the rich, the poor, the oppressed, the marginalized, and the despised to come together and transform this world for the Kingdom of God. The question is which campaign are you going to support? Will you support Satan, the campaign of the prince of this world, or the campaign of Jesus Christ? You cannot support both of them. This is not a political game of which

---

[9] Or *the gospel*

7

money can be used for favors, and special interest groups can buy votes. At least not with the campaign ministry of Jesus Christ. You can only work in one campaign. Jesus said, " No one can serve two masters; for either he will hate the one and love the other, or he will be devoted to one and despise the other." (Matthew 6:24) Only one can sit on the throne of your heart and live in the oval office of your soul.

You must understand that the battle between the two Kingdoms is spiritual and revolutionary. "For our wrestling[10] is not against flesh and blood, but against the rulers, against the powers, against the world-rulers of this darkness, against the wicked spirit forces in the heavenly places." (Ephesians 6:12) Social and economic structures are not going to transform themselves, and to attempt to transform them for the Kingdom of God means fierce opposition and possibly death. The call to follow Jesus Christ is a call to go against structural oppression that legitimates a caste system that keeps people divided and marginalized. The ethics, values and principles that Jesus is calling you to embrace are diametrically opposed to the structural systems of this world. In short, this journey is dangerous because it could get you killed for trying to apply principles of a Kingdom that are not of this world. (John 18:36) It is difficult to hear the word killed because we love this life. However, this is the very life Jesus is asking you to give up to follow him. To follow Jesus is to be cemetery ready. Yes, this means to expect becoming a martyr if necessary for the cause of Jesus Christ. Anyone who decides to follow Jesus on this journey must be prepared to die.

Therefore, before you enlist to join Jesus and are deployed to engage in spiritual warfare know and understand the cost. Following Jesus Christ is not a fairytale journey nor is it for the fainthearted. Jesus declared, "For whoever would

---

[10] Or struggle

save his soul[11] will lose it, but whoever loses his soul[12] for my sake will find it." (Matthew 16:25) Like anyone who joins the armed forces must be prepared to make the ultimate sacrifice; so it is with joining Jesus Christ. You must be willing to suffer on the journey and lay down your life for Jesus who declared to be the "Way, the Truth and the Life." Dietrich Bonhoeffer hits the nail on the head, "When Christ calls a man he bids him to come and die."[13] The call to follow Jesus Christ is a death march, which means taking up one's cross and undergoing the pain, suffering, and rejection this world will heap upon you. The call is for all people, all tongues, and all languages who want to enter and live eternally in the Kingdom of God. This is the reason followers of Christ should not allow racial, educational, cultural, denominational, economic and social differences to divide them. Followers are on the same team inculcated with the same Spirit that gave Jesus victory over sin, death, and the grave.

Make no mistake about it; Jesus is not inviting you on this journey of which there is ease, comfort, and hazard free traveling. To follow Jesus means suffering, persecution, insults, rejection, name-calling, imprisonment, ejection from the church and physical death. It is not a matter of if this will happen to followers of Jesus Christ but when. This is the reason very few people make the journey. This is why many turn back when criticism, opposition, persecution, and death comes. They did not count the cost. The cost is not just attending church for an hour or two on Sunday. It is not just attending Bible study and volunteering time at church through the week. It is not just helping out at a mission site. As important as these things are, the cost of following Jesus involves much more than this. The cost is death, and most people don't want to pay this price. But, you must die to

---

[11] I.e., *life*

[12] I.e., *life*

[13] Dietrich Bonhoeffer, *The Cost of Discipleship*, Collier Books, 1963, 99.

yourself and come alive in Jesus Christ to be his life, arms, legs, and voice in a world that is existentially broken, fragmented and alienated from God; a world of which the culture is so psychologically, pathologically, and spiritually sick that a follower of Jesus Christ may panic when the pressures of this pilgrimage set in.

Jesus wants you to understand the cost before you venture onto the journey with him. The crowd that followed Jesus had not counted the cost. They thought Jesus was going to set up a material Kingdom by overthrowing Roman rule setting Jerusalem free from tyranny and oppression. However, Jesus had them to know what his real mission was in the world, and before they set out to follow him, they ought to first count the cost. Jesus said, "For which one of you when he wants to build a tower, does not first sit down and calculate the cost to see if he has enough to complete it? Otherwise, when he has laid a foundation and is not able to finish, all who see it begin to ridicule him, saying, 'This man began to build and was not able to finish.' Or what king, going out to encounter another king in war, will not sit down first and deliberate whether he is able with ten thousand to meet the one coming against him with twenty thousand." (Luke 14:28-31) You should know what you are getting into when you decide to follow Christ. To follow Christ is not an easy road to travel. This road is narrow, and it gets lonely sometimes, it gets dark sometimes; it has twists and turns; and ultimately a road that is headed toward crucifixion. If you are serious about following Christ, count the cost, and pick up your cross and follow him daily.

Many people say they want to follow Christ. They hear the clarion call; the preaching and teaching of the Word move them; they are on an emotional high. They decide to give their lives to Christ with the intention of following him. Soon they find out what it cost, how much commitment is involved, how much sacrifice it entails, and many fall away. They were not willing to pay the cost of responsibility and

10

commitment the journey demands. To follow Christ is more than just having a church, followers must be the church. It means you must practice self-denial; you must be willing to give up everything and not hold back anything. You must be willing to face danger; you must endure criticism, persecution, indignities, and all of the harsh realities of being a disciple. These things will come when you truly decide to follow Jesus. However, remember whatever Christ leads you to do he can lead you through. Followers must be willing to give up all in order to have all in Jesus Christ. The rich young ruler went away sorrowful because not only did he have great wealth, his wealth had him (Matthew 19:22). He saw the right road but turned away from it. He came to the right person but refused to follow him. He sought life but chose death. To follow Jesus Christ, you must be willing to give up everything. Jesus discouraged any person who was half-hearted or lukewarm about following him. He wanted it known that he is not seeking fans, admirers, and people who have ulterior motives for following him. Jesus makes hard demands on followers, and if you are not willing to meet these demands, you cannot be his disciple. You may have confessed him, attend church, give your offering, serve in some ministry, but you cannot be his disciple because he is not your only priority. Unless he is your only priority, you are looking to be a fan, not a follower.

One day a mother came to Jesus and said unto him, "'Say that these two sons of mine are to sit, one at your right hand and one at your left, in your kingdom.' But Jesus answered, 'You do not know what you are asking. Are you able to drink the cup that I am to drink?'" (Matthew 20:20-23) Jesus was saying to this mother as he is saying to anyone who wants to follow him. Can you drink the cup of sacrifice and be baptized in the water of self-denial? You must remember the way of the cross is not about position, titles, status, and celebrity. To follow Christ is going to cost you everything. If you desire to follow Jesus Christ, save yourself some time, stress, and disappointment and consider the cost. Jesus said, "If anyone comes to me and does not hate his own father and mother and wife and children and brothers and sisters, yes, and even his own life, he cannot be my disciple. Whoever does not carry his own cross and come after me cannot be my disciple."[14] (Luke 14:26-27) Wait a minute! Is Jesus literally asking people to consider what he just said to follow him? Absolutely! Not only does Jesus want you to consider this but willing to do this to be his disciple. Regardless of what you have been taught about Christianity, to follow Jesus Christ is no blissful fantasy of ease and comfort in this morally dark world. Too many Christians have been misled or misinformed in their Bible education and fed a sedative gospel of which they expect material gain, ease, comfort, and popularity but no suffering and sacrifice. Some say, "Jesus has suffered, and we don't have to." Those who say this do not know Scripture. "Indeed, all who desire to live godly in Christ Jesus will be persecuted." (2 Timothy 3:12) Jesus does not want you caught off-guard or surprised that suffering and sacrifice are part of the journey with him. This is why the cross and self-denial are so crucial in understanding what to expect following Jesus. This is not to suggest we take a vow of poverty and go around with a martyr complex. However, you are to be ready at all times to do the will of God and not your own. You have been "Bought with a price." (1 Corinthians 6:20) which means you do not belong to yourself but to him who purchased you with his blood.

It is not easy to deny and slay yourself in order to follow Jesus. It is not easy to choose Jesus over culture, friends,

---

[14] **How are we to understand that Christians are to "hate" their relatives?** In the Scriptures, "hate" often refers to loving a person or an object less than another person or object. (Gen. 29:30-31) In other words, those following Christ are to "hate" their relative, in that they are to love them less that they love Jesus. (Matt 10:37)

money, materialism, promotions, popularity, power, privilege, and especially family. Sometimes, all we have in this world is family. People often say, "Blood is thicker than water." But, to follow Jesus obedience is thicker than blood. Therefore, before you sign up to follow Jesus, first consider the cost. "In a world where everything revolves around self—protect yourself, promote yourself, preserve yourself, entertain yourself, comfort yourself, take care of yourself—Jesus said, "Slay yourself.""[15] To follow Jesus means to remove yourself from the center of your life and make Jesus the center of your life. The question is can you handle removing yourself from sitting on the throne of your heart and allow Jesus to sit there instead? Can you handle entering into human suffering to help provide relief to hurting humanity? Can you handle rejection, biting criticism, and harsh misunderstanding that inevitably comes from following Jesus? Can you handle persecution as a result of following Jesus? Can you handle the possibility of losing your life for the cause of Jesus Christ?

These questions are not easy to answer, but they are necessary to consider before you enlist to follow Jesus. Too many Christians fail to read the fine print before they enlist to follow Jesus. "For many Christians the concept of denying themselves was not part of the deal. They grew up with the message that such a radical decision really isn't necessary. So they signed up to follow Jesus, but if denying themselves was part of the explanation, it was definitely the fine print. That's especially true of American Christians. In part, this is due to the collision of Christianity with American capitalism. It has created a culture of consumers in our churches. Instead of approaching their faith with a spirit of denial that says, 'What can I do for Jesus?" they have a consumer mentality that says,

---

[15] David Platt, What Did Jesus Really Mean When He Said Follow Me, Tyndale House Publisher, 2013, 19.

'What can Jesus do for me?"[16] So many Christians come to church with a give me mentality that overlooks a servant mentality. What people must understand is Jesus Christ has given his life for humanity, and he is not a bellhop waiting to give us material possessions that may trump our relationship with him and stifle our commitment to the work of the Kingdom of God. Jesus Christ is ready to strengthen and replenish us on this journey as we follow him in doing the will of God on earth as it is in heaven. This explanation is not a case against material blessings. It is a case of priority and alignment. Our priority must first be the Kingdom of God. Jesus said, "But be you seeking[17] the kingdom of God and his righteousness, and all these things will be added to you." (Matthew 6:33) We must be correctly aligned vertically and horizontally with the Kingdom of God, continuously. It is something that we must do up unto our death or until the second coming of Christ, whichever comes first.

Not only does this journey requires that you deny yourself to follow Jesus, but it also requires at times enduring the profound loneliness of living a countercultural life in a world that is spiritually and morally bankrupt. It means to live a diametrically opposite life among people who are spiritually blind, and who don't care about God and His kingdom. It means living out the principles of the Kingdom of God in a world that sees these principles as weak and foolish, and scoffs at the Christian faith and ethics. To follow Jesus is to make the kingdom of God top priority because God's Kingdom and the Kingdom of this world are polar opposites. Satan, the evil one is the leader of the Kingdom of this world, and his objective is to kill, steal, and destroy. On the other hand, Jesus the leader of the Kingdom of God, objective is to give life and give it more abundantly (John 10:10)." There

---

[16] Kyle Idleman, Not a Fan Becoming a Completely Committed Follower of Jesus, Zondervan, 2011, 148.

[17] Gr., *zeteite*; the verb form indicates continuous action.

14

will always be a clash or collision with the two Kingdoms. Both Kingdoms are different in ethics, values, and principles. There will never be a collaboration between the Kingdom of light and the kingdom of darkness. There will never be a compromise with the two Kingdoms. Both Kingdoms have clear objectives. One leads to death, and one leads to life. One leads us away from God, and one leads us to God. There is no gray area between the two kingdoms.

However, "As soon as Christ's Kingdom comes to terms with the world, Christianity is abolished. If on the other hand, Christ is the truth, His is truly enough a Kingdom in this world, but not of this world, that is to say, it is militant. . . . To be a Christian in this militant Church means to express what it is to be a Christian within an environment which is the opposite to Christian."[18] The militant Church struggles to be true to its King, and regardless of the threats and persecutions it suffers, the militant church does not compromise with the Kingdom of this world. It does not lower its standards to accommodate the Kingdom of this world. "So long as this world endures or so long as the Christian Church shall exist in this world, it is and should be a militant Church."[19] This militancy is not a physical war with our taking up carnal weapons against the world, but rather it is the Holy Spirit operating in and through followers of Jesus Christ to accomplish the goal of the Kingdom of God, and that is "not wishing for any to perish but for all to come to repentance." (2 Peter 3:9)

The reason the postmodern church has become ineffective is its practice of lukewarmness. Many Christians are not exclusively for the Kingdom of God nor the Kingdom of this world. They are not truly loyal to either one. They make too many compromises and seek peace and friendship between the two Kingdoms. Soren Kierkegaard warns, "The

---

[18] Soren Kierkegaard, Training in Christianity, 207.
[19] Ibid., 215

day when Christianity and the world becomes friends Christianity is done away with."[20] Christianity loses its focus and its power, and stands in danger of having its candlestick moved out of its place (Revelation 2:5) when it desires peace and friendship with the world. Christ did not come in the world to make peace between the two Kingdoms. Jesus said, "Do not think that I came to bring peace on earth. I did not come to bring peace but a sword. For I have come to set a man against his father, a daughter against her mother, and a daughter-in-law against her mother-in-law, and a [follower's] enemies will be those of his own household (Matthew 10:34-36.)" Jesus did not come to make friendship with this world and neither should his followers. "Christ came to the world for purpose of saving the world, and at the same time (as was implied in His first purpose) to be 'the pattern,' to leave behind Him footsteps for those who would attach themselves to Him, who thus might become followers, for 'follower' corresponds to 'footsteps.'[21] To follow Jesus is to correspond to his footsteps and be exclusively for the Kingdom of God and totally against Satan and the Kingdom of this world. Will this be easy? No! Will this require great sacrifice? Yes! Does it mean persecution and death? Yes! What is the reward at the end of this Christian journey? The reward is eternal life with Jesus Christ in the Kingdom of God; a Kingdom of which there is no end! Jesus wants you to know about this journey with him before you set out to follow him. This journey entails mountaintop and valley experiences, storms and periods of sunshine, ebb and flow of joy and sorrow, some acceptance but most rejection of people. Regardless of the present situation you find yourself in on the journey, to obtain eternal life, you must remain faithful on the journey wherever it leads you and whatever happens to you.

---

[20] Ibid., 218-219.
[21] Ibid, 232.

The greatest struggle on the journey will be with yourself. Denying yourself and becoming totally committed to Jesus will be the greatest battle. Dealing with other people and their resistance is tough enough, but the toughest challenge is with yourself. To bring your heart and mind under the authority and obedience of Jesus Christ is very difficult. The principles that Jesus taught are not only ridiculous to the world, but at times will be unacceptable to you, especially when your flesh becomes weak and discouragement sets in. This is why you must have faith on this journey because dark clouds will come; the winds of adversity will blow, and human rationale and emotion will tempt you to turn back from following Jesus. Just like an airplane pilot in a violent storm must not rely on his feelings but must trust his instruments to get him through a storm, so it is in following Jesus. You must not rely on your feelings, emotions, and human rationale to guide you on this journey. Your trust must be in Jesus Christ who promised: "Never to leave you never to leave you alone." Just like baby ducks follow their leader wherever she goes without regard for danger and death, you must likewise follow Jesus.

The journey with Jesus is the most important decision you can make in life, and once the decision is made to follow him, the reward outweighs anything this world can offer. Jesus taught, "For what does it profit a man to gain the whole world and forfeit his soul? For what can a man give in exchange for his soul? (Mark 8:36-37) We cannot and will not lose making a lifelong investment with the Son of God. It would be a stupid and foolish trade-off not to follow Christ because, at the end of this age when all nations have to stand before the judgment seat of Christ, no amount of money, education, position, political party, and security can save you. If you have made an investment in this world and not in Jesus Christ, you will lose your soul. But, to follow Jesus will cost you your life, your will, your way, your security, and your wellbeing. This is a small sacrifice in comparison to eternal rewards. Paul writes about the reward waiting for those who finished the journey with Jesus Christ, "Things which eye has not seen and ear has not heard, and have not entered into the heart of man, all that God has prepared for those who love him." (1 Corinthians 2:9) What God has through Jesus Christ is so magnificent and awe-stricken it has not been revealed in human imagination.

However, in order to be a recipient of that which has not been revealed for those who love the Lord, you must live a totally surrendered life to Jesus. You must be willing to live as Jesus lived; go where Jesus goes; serve like Jesus serves; love like Jesus loves; forgive like Jesus forgives; and obey like Jesus obeyed. The question is, are you willing to take the journey with Jesus? Before you make your decision, please understand that the journey is dangerous; you will be tested and tried; you will be a target for the enemy; you will experience temptation, rejection, criticism, loneliness; betrayal; persecution, and a host of other unpleasant realities from an evil and unbelieving world. Only those who are rooted and grounded in Christ will complete the journey. Jesus will not accept any excuses if you are lost in the end. There is no excuse for putting off following Jesus. There is no excuse for not obeying the Gospel of Jesus Christ. Those who make excuses will not be in the fellowship with Jesus Christ nor taste his eternal life in the Kingdom to come. (Luke 14:16-24) So, make up your mind today and not wait until tomorrow. Tomorrow may never come.

If you are willing to follow and become a disciple of Jesus Christ, the following chapters will describe what to expect on this journey, and each chapter will end with an encouraging hymn to help you stay on the journey. Chapter 1 describes Jesus, our inconvenient leader. Chapter 2 prepares you for temptation. Chapter 3 prepares you for rejection. Chapter 4 prepares you for criticism. Chapter 5 prepares you for loneliness. Chapter 6 prepares you for betrayal. Chapter 7 prepares you for persecution. Chapter 8 prepares you for death. Chapter Nine prepares you for the great reward. Chapter 10 concludes with Christians examining themselves to see if they are followers of Jesus Christ or the culture. Either Christians are going to be thermostats that set the temperature of society or thermometers that only register the temperature. If today's Christians have not experienced the cross and all it entails, then they are not following Christ.

My hope and prayer is that this book would give you a raw outlook on following Christ and disturb the slumbering conscience of those who claim to be Christians. It is not my intention to give you a snuggly and cozy description of following Jesus Christ. You would lose heart on the journey when the truth emerges. I want you to understand following Jesus Christ is not like being on a cruise ship; it is like being on a battleship where you are engaged in spiritual warfare of which the enemy will be shooting fiery darts at you. On the journey, the enemy will try to kill, steal, and destroy you. The battleship you are on will rock from side to side. Don't panic because Jesus is the captain, and if you stick with him on the journey, you will arrive at your destination of eternal life. It is better to know what you are getting into with your eyes wide open than with blind assumptions on the journey. One thing is sure when you decide to follow Jesus; your life will never be the same. Jesus gives peace beyond understanding, and joy unspeakable joy. Although the journey will be rough at times, remember Jesus promised never to leave you never to leave you alone! This is a hymn to remember on this journey by George A. Young, "God Leads Us Along."

> In shady, green pastures, so rich and so sweet,
> God leads
> His dear children along;
> Where the water's cool flow bathes the weary
> one's feet
> God leads His dear children along.

Some though the waters, some through the flood,

Some through the fire, but all through the blood;

Some through great sorrow, but God gives a song,

In the night season and all the day long.

Sometimes on the mount where the sun shines so bright

God leads His dear children along;

Sometimes in the valley, in darkest of night,

God leads His dear children along.

(3) Tho' sorrow befall us and Satan oppose,

God leads His dear children along;

Thru grace we can conquer, defeat all our foes,

God leads His dear children along!

Away from the mire and away from the clay,

God leads His dear children along;

Away up in glory, eternity's day.

God leads His dear children along!

Some thru the waters, some through the flood,

Some through the fire, but all through the blood;

Some through great sorrow, but God gives a song,

In the night season, and all the day long.[22]

---

[22] George A. Young, "God Leads Us Along" copyright 1963.

CHAPTER ONE Jesus the Inconvenient Leader

> Life was very inconvenient for the Savior, and, I believe it will often be so for us when we take upon his name.—Jeffrey R. Holland

Before following any leader, you should know as much as you can about the leader. You should go through a vetting process to know the leader's background, experience, and as many facts about the leader before you set out to follow. Can the leader be trusted? What are the leader's character and personality? Learn about the leader's mission and goal? Before you embark upon a journey to follow a leader, learn all you can about the leader. You should never blindly follow a leader because this can be destructive. Remember in 1978 Jim Jones who led a mass murder-suicide in Jonestown Guyana. You must be extremely careful who you follow because many false prophets are in the world transforming themselves as angels of light. Since Jesus Christ is the leader on this dangerous Christian journey, he encourages people to "Learn from me, for I am gentle and lowly in heart, and you will find rest for your souls. 30 For my yoke is easy,[23] and my burden is light." (Matthew 11:29-30) To learn of Jesus is to see how transparent and consistent he is. "Jesus Christ is the same yesterday and today, and forever. (Hebrews 13:8) You won't have to worry about him changing. Time and circumstances will not cause Jesus to change. He is the same forever. Once you have studied, assessed, and evaluated Jesus, you must make the decision to follow him. You must put your total trust in him. Trust is major on this dangerous journey. Without trust you cannot complete the journey. Trust in Jesus Christ doesn't mean you will understand

---

[23] I.e. *easy to bear*

everything on the journey; trust in Jesus means you continue on the journey even when you cannot comprehend all the twists and turns, curves and embankments you encounter on the journey.

To journey with Jesus, you must first let go of all attachments to this world. There should be no unfinished business with the world. Hazrat Inayat Khan gives deep insight about starting this journey. "If there is anything a man has not learned, he must finish it before starting the journey, for if he thinks, 'I will start the journey, although I had the desire to learn something before starting,' in that case he will not be able to reach his goal. That desire to learn something will draw him back. Every desire, every ambition, every aspiration that he has in life must be gratified. Not only this, man must have no remorse of any kind when starting on this journey and no repentance afterwards. If there is any repentance or remorse it must be finished before starting. There must be no grudge against anybody, and no complaining of anyone having done him harm, for all these things, which belong to this world, if man took them along, would become a burden on the spiritual path. The journey is difficult enough, and it becomes more difficult if there is a burden to be carried."[24]

Jesus said, "No man who puts his hand to the plow and looks back is fit for the kingdom of God." (Luke 9:62) So, once you make the decision to follow Jesus, you must never look back. You must follow him during the good times as well as the bad times, during times of plenty and times of scarcity, during times of praise and times of harsh criticism, and times when facing physical death. Death is the ultimate sacrifice. If you are unwilling to give up this physical life with all of its material comforts, you cannot really be a disciple of Jesus Christ in the new life he offers. Whatever situations and

---

[24] Hazrat Inayat Khan, The Inner Life, Shambhala Publications, 1997, 4.

circumstances you find yourself in while following Christ, you must continue the journey at all cost. You must remember that following Christ won't be a convenient journey because you are led by an inconvenient leader who makes inconvenient demands on followers. Those demands will go against your feelings, your culture, your traditions, and those things you hold dear to your heart. Because Jesus was rejected, despised, and finally crucified, this will be your lot as well. Maybe not in the exact same way as Jesus and on the same level but you will undergo what the Apostle Paul called "momentary and light afflictions." (2 Corinthians 4:17)

Regardless of how the church, books, and preachers have tried to sanitize and tone down or mitigate the life of Jesus to make him more palatable, safe, and non-offensive, the historical facts show that he was an inconvenient leader who did not bite his tongue, sugar coat his message, and not afraid to disturb the religious and political establishment. John MacArthur says of Jesus, "Nothing He said about the cost of discipleship was ever toned down, dumbed down, lightened up, glossed over, mitigated, understated, or pillowed in soft words. He was not the least bit encouraging toward people who wanted to follow Him around just for the food and the miracles. In fact, He did everything possible to discourage people like that (John 6)."[25] Jesus was outright dangerous in his day. He disturbs things that were out of the compliance with the will of God. In short, he was a revolutionist. Henri J.M. Nouwen said, "Jesus was a revolutionary, who did not become an extremist since he did not offer an ideology, but Himself. He was also a mystic, who did not use his intimate relationship with God to avoid the social evils of his time but shocked his milieu to the point of being executed as a rebel. In this sense he also remains for nuclear man the way to

---

[25] John MacArthur, The Gospel According to Jesus, Zondervan, 31-32.

liberation and freedom."[26] Diarmaid O'Murchu advances the true history of Jesus. "Jesus lived dangerously! He did not fit into the conventional culture of his day. He questioned many of its core beliefs. He sought to empower the marginalized and oppressed. In addition, he paid the ultimate price for living so dangerously. Being the rebel he was, the countercultural prophet, largely misunderstood in his own time and culture, it is quite amazing that he found a place in mainline history."[27]

MACCABEAN EXCURSION

CHRISTIAN PUBLISHING HOUSE: Was Jesus a rebel? A rebel is **(1)** somebody who rejects the codes and conventions of society, **(2)** to rise in opposition or armed resistance to an established government or ruler **(3)** a soldier who belongs to a force seeking to overthrow a government or ruling power, **(4)** somebody who defiantly protests against authority.

The above from Dr. Davis is historically accurate; however, we have to be very careful when saying, "Jesus was a rebel." Why? The word "rebel" means different things to different people and segments of society. Technically speaking Satan was the first rebel, who then caused Eve and then Adam to join his rebellion against God. A rebel simply rebels against a person, group or organization that is in a position of authority or power. Now, in some ways, this could be a good thing and at other times, this could be a bad thing. A rebel could be a peaceful demonstration against a person, group or

---

[26] Henri J.M. Nouwen, The Wounded Healer, Image Books: A Division of Doubleday & Company, 1979, 20-21.

[27] Diarmaid O'murchu, Christianity's Dangerous Memory, A Rediscovery of the Revolutionary Jesus, The Crossroad Publishing Company, 2011, 1.

24

organization in power because they are perceived as doing something wrong. However, in reviewing the United States in 2016, it can also be young people joining together by the thousands to rise up in rebellion against authority, tearing apart and burning down communities, carrying out violence on innocent citizens to make some kind of social justice or political point.

Without the historical setting of Jesus' life and ministry, we could actually misconstrue his rebellion against the Judaism of the time. Very briefly, we will cover the historical setting of Jesus. We are going to go back to the period of the rise and the fall of the Maccabees, which comes after the book of Malachi but before the time of Matthew's Gospel. Who were the Maccabees? How did they bring about the transformation of the Israelites of the Old Testament into the Judaism before the coming of the foretold Messiah?

The brief history below are from different sources, however the chart is by Edward D. Andrews.

The Maccabees

After the Jewish people's return from Babylonian Exile in 536 B.C., for a time they were able to restore pure worship because they return to God. However, ...

In Judea the Jewish people were ruled by governors who held office at the pleasure of the Persian king. One of the earlier governors was Zerubbabel (Hg 1:1; 2:1), a descendant of David (1 Chr 3:10–19). In some way he shared rule with the high priest Jeshua ben Jehozadak. Palestine was part of one of the 20 satrapies of the Persian Empire, which lasted from 539 to 331 B.C., when it fell to the Greeks under Alexander the Great. Little is known about the historical developments in Palestine during most of the Persian period. When Alexander died in 323 B.C., his empire was divided up among his generals; Egypt and Palestine fell to Ptolemy I. The Ptolemies were benevolent despots who allowed the Jews of Palestine a measure of freedom and autonomy. After the battle of Paneion in 198 B.C., Palestine came under the rule of the Seleucid Empire, founded by Seleucus I, another of Alexander's generals.

The Seleucid Empire embraced a very large area with a diverse population, extending from Asia Minor and Palestine in the west to the borders of India on the east. Antiochus IV (Epiphanes) ascended the Seleucid throne in 175 B.C. and attempted to unify his vast empire by Hellenizing it (i.e., by forcing the adoption of Greek language and culture). Local cultures and religions were forcibly suppressed as a result of this policy, and the Jewish state in Palestine was perhaps the hardest hit of all. In 167 B.C. Antiochus IV dedicated the temple in Jerusalem to Olympian Zeus, sacrificed a sow on the altar, destroyed scrolls containing the Jewish Scriptures, and forbade the rite of circumcision. This repression triggered a revolt led by an aged priest named Mattathias and his sons. The Seleucids were repulsed, and finally in 164 b.c. the temple was retaken by Mattathias' son Judas the Maccabee (an epithet meaning "the hammer"). This Jewish victory has been commemorated annually by the festival of Hanukkah ("dedication"). Judas and his brothers, called Maccabees or Hasmoneans (Mattathias was of the house of Hasmon), and their descendants ruled Judea from 164 to 63, when Palestine fell to the Roman general Pompey. Thereafter, Palestine remained a vassal of Rome.

Hyrcanus, a Hasmonean, was high priest after the conquest of Judea by the Romans, though Antipater, an Idumean, was the real power behind Hyrcanus. The sons of Antipater, Phasael and Herod, were governors of Jerusalem and Galilee, respectively. Upon the assassination of

Antipater in 43 B.C., and through his connections in Rome, Herod (later called Herod the Great) was named king of Judea by the Roman senate; he reigned from 37 to 4 b.c. When he died, Palestine was divided up by the emperor Augustus (27 B.C.–A.D. 14) and placed under the governorship of three of Herod's sons: Herod Archelaus (ethnarch of Judea, Idumaea, and Samaria from 4 B.C. to A.D. 6), Herod Antipas (tetrarch of Galilee and Perea from 4 B.C. to A.D. 39), and Herod Philip (tetrarch of Batanea, Trachonitis, and other small states from 4 B.C. to A.D. 34). These territories were generally placed under Roman procurators after the sons of Herod had died or been deposed. For a brief period (a.d. 41–44), Herod Agrippa I, the grandson of Herod the Great, ruled virtually the same territory as his grandfather. Upon his death (narrated in Acts 12:20–23), his territories were placed under Roman procurators. The greed and ineptness of these procurators provoked the Jewish populace to rebel. The illfated Jewish revolt of A.D. 66–73 resulted in the destruction of the second temple by the Tenth Roman legion under Titus in 70. The revolt was completely quelled in 73, when more than 900 Jews under siege in the desert fortress of Masada near the Dead Sea committed mass suicide rather than fall into Roman hands. These tragic events ended permanently the temple cult and the priestly system in Judaism.[28]

---

[28] Walter A. Elwell and Barry J. Beitzel, *Baker Encyclopedia of the Bible* (Grand Rapids, MI: Baker Book House, 1988), 1230–1231.

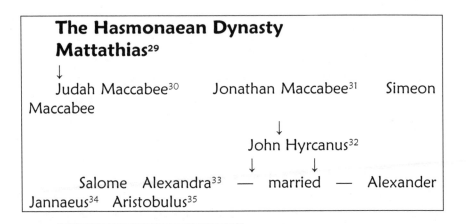

The Hasmonaean Dynasty
Mattathias[29]

↓

Judah Maccabee[30]   Jonathan Maccabee[31]   Simeon Maccabee

↓

John Hyrcanus[32]

↓   ↓

Salome Alexandra[33] — married — Alexander

Jannaeus[34] Aristobulus[35]

---

[29] Mattathias defies attempts by the Seleucid leader Antiochus IV to Hellenize the Jews in 167 B.C.E. He dies one year later, and his son Judah Maccabee takes his place.

[30] In 166 B.C.E., Judah defeats the Seleucid army at Beth Horon and Emmaus. In 164 B.C.E. Antiochus IV dies and is succeeded by Antiochus V. In 164 B.C.E., Judah defeats the Seleucid army at Beth Zur and captures Jerusalem, reconsecrating the temple. In 162 B.C.E., Demetrius I takes the Seleucid throne. In 161 B.C.E., the Maccabees defeat the Seleucids at Adasa. In 160 B.C.E., the Seleucids defeat the Maccabees and Judah was killed in the battle, with Jonathan taking his place as the leader.

[31] In 157 B.C.E., the Seleucids recognize Jonathan Maccabee as a minor king within their empire. In 152 B.C.E., Jonathan withdraws support from Demetrius and gives it to Alexander Balas, a pretender to the Seleucid throne. Jonathan becomes high priest. In 150 B.C.E., Alexander Balas defeats Demetrius and becomes ruler of the Seleucid Empire. In 145, B.C.E. Alexander Balas is killed and is succeeded by Demetrius' son, Demetrius' II. In 142 B.C.E., Jonathan is killed and succeeded by Simeon Maccabee as high priest. Simeon renewed the alliance with Rome. In 141 B.C.E., the Seleucids surrender Jerusalem, with Simeon becoming ruler of Judea. In 135 B.C.E., Simeon is killed and is succeeded by John Hyrcanus.

[32] John Hyrcanus succeeds Simeon when he is killed in 135 B.C.E.

[33] Salome Alexandra proved herself a accomplished ruler, giving Israel one of the more peaceful periods under Hasmonaean rule (76-67 B.C.E.). The Pharisees were returned to positions of authority, and the laws against their religious decrees were revoked.

[34] In 103 B.C.E., Aristobulus I dies and is succeeded his brother Alexander Jannaeus. Jannaeus was a reasonable politician. He saw that

$\downarrow$ $\downarrow$

Hyrcanus II[36]   Aristobulus II

The Maccabees restored worship at the temple before the coming of the Messiah. (See John 1:41-42; 2:13-17) However, just as purity of worship was debased by the actions of Hellenized priests, it became even worse by the end of the Hasmonaean dynasty. To be sure, rule by priests, who were politically minded as opposed to a king of faithful David's line, resulted in the Jewish people rejecting the long awaited Messiah, Jesus Christ. (2 Samuel 7:16; Psalm 89:3-4, 35-36)

Pharisees and Sadducees Appear

Pharisees The Pharisees constituted the largest and most important group, Josephus stating that they numbered about 6,000. They appear in the Gospels as opponents of Jesus. Paul was a Pharisee (Phil. 3:5). They controlled the synagogues and exercised great control over much of the

---

the Pharisees had growing widespread support. Alexander broke with preceding policy and without restrictions declared himself both high priest and king. The battles between the Hasmonaeans and the Pharisees increased, even leading to a civil war, where 50,000 Jews were killed. His dying instruction to his wife, Salome Alexandra, was to divide power with them. Jannaeus had selected her over his sons as replacement to his kingdom.

[35] In 104 B.C.E., Aristobulus I succeeds John Hyrcanus.

[36] When Salome died, her two sons Hyrcanus II, who had served as high priest and Aristobulus II, began a struggle for power. Neither has the political or military practical understanding of their forefathers. They were simply oblivious to the growing power of the Roman Empire. In 63 B.C.E., both Hyrcanus II and Aristobulus II sought the help of the Roman ruler Pompey while he was in Damascus, seeking his intervention in their quarrel of power. However, it was this same year that Pompey marched into Jerusalem with his troops, taking control, which meant the end of the Hasmonaean kingdom.

population.

No surviving writing gives us information about the origin of the Pharisees. The earliest reference to them is in the time of Jonathan (160–143 b.c.) when Josephus refers to Pharisees, Sadducees, and Essenes. Their good relations with the rulers ended in the time of John Hyrcanus (134–104 B.C.). They came to power again when Salome Alexandra became Queen (76 B.C.).

The term "Pharisee" means, "separated ones." Perhaps it means that they separated themselves from the masses or that they separated themselves to the study and interpretation of the law. A common assumption is that they developed from the Hasidim, the ultra-orthodox loyal freedom fighters in the time of Judas Maccabeus. They apparently were responsible for the transformation of Judaism from a religion of sacrifice to one of law. They were the developers of the oral tradition, the teachers of the two-fold law: written and oral. They saw the way to God as being through obedience to the law. They were the progressives of the day, willing to adopt new ideas and adapt the law to new situations.

The Pharisees were strongly monotheistic. They accepted all the OT as authoritative. They affirmed the reality of angels and demons. They had a firm belief in life beyond the grave and a resurrection of the body. They were missionary, seeking the conversion of Gentiles (Matt. 23:15). They saw God as concerned with the life of a person without denying that the individual was responsible for how he or she lived. They had little interest in politics. The Pharisees opposed Jesus because He refused to accept their interpretations of the oral law.[37]

---

[37] Charles W. Draper with Harrop Clayton, "Jewish Parties in the New Testament," ed. Chad Brand et al., *Holman Illustrated Bible Dictionary* (Nashville, TN: Holman Bible Publishers, 2003), 916–917.

Sadducees The Sadducees were aristocrats. They were the party of the wealthy and of the high priestly families. They were in charge of the temple, its services, and concessions. They claimed to be descendants of Zadok, high priest of Solomon. True derivation of the term is unknown. In all our literature they stand in opposition to the Pharisees. They were social conservatives, seeking to preserve the practices of the past. They opposed the oral law, accepting the Pentateuch as the ultimate authority. The Sadducees were materialistic in their outlook. They did not believe in life after death or rewards or punishment beyond this life. They denied the existence of angels and demons. They did not believe that God was concerned with what people did. Rather, people were totally free. They were politically oriented, supporters of ruling powers, whether Seleucids or Romans. They tolerated no threats to their position and wealth, so they strongly opposed Jesus.[38]

Herodians The Herodians are mentioned only three times in the NT (Matt. 22:16; Mark 3:6; 12:13). In Mark they joined the Pharisees in a plot to kill Jesus. The other references are to Pharisees and Herodians together asking Jesus about paying taxes to Caesar. They were Jews who supported Herod Antipas or sought to have a descendant of Herod the Great given authority over Palestine. At this time Judea and Samaria were under Roman governors.[39]

Zealots The Zealots are mentioned rarely in the NT. Simon, one of the disciples, is called Zealot (Luke 6:15). John 18:40 uses a word for Barabbas that Josephus used for Zealot. Josephus said the Zealots began with Judas the

[38] Charles W. Draper with Harrop Clayton, "Jewish Parties in the New Testament," ed. Chad Brand et al., *Holman Illustrated Bible Dictionary* (Nashville, TN: Holman Bible Publishers, 2003), 917.

[39] Charles W. Draper with Harrop Clayton, "Jewish Parties in the New Testament," ed. Chad Brand et al., *Holman Illustrated Bible Dictionary* (Nashville, TN: Holman Bible Publishers, 2003), 917.

Galilean seeking to lead a revolt over a taxation census (a.d. 6). He did not use the name Zealot until referring to events in a.d. 66, the first Jewish revolt against Rome. The Zealots were the extreme wing of the Pharisees. In contrast with other Pharisees they believed only God had the right to rule over the Jews. They were willing to fight and die for that belief. For them nationalistic patriotism and religion were inseparable.[40]

Sicarii Literally meaning "dagger men," the Sicarii were the most extreme revolutionaries among the Jews of the first century. Committed to the overthrow of Roman power over Palestine, they used small concealed daggers to assassinate their enemies, principally Roman officials. They were willing to die in killing their targets and did whatever they could to disrupt Roman political and military policy.[41]

Again, in short, Jesus was born into a world where the Roman Empire ruled the then known world. Roman wisely allowed different parts of the empire to keep their own religious and cultural beliefs as long as they did not go against Rome. Within Palestine, especially the Jerusalem area the Pharisees and Sadducees oppressed the Jewish people with their oral law. This oral law was not based on the Hebrew Old Testament Scriptures but rather it was the twisted interpretation of the Jewish Rabbis (i.e., teachers). Jesus did not rebel against the Roman government. However, in a sense, he did rebel against the Judaism of his day. Nonetheless, Jesus did not rise in opposition or armed resistance to Judaism seeking to overthrow the Jewish

---

[40] Charles W. Draper with Harrop Clayton, "Jewish Parties in the New Testament," ed. Chad Brand et al., *Holman Illustrated Bible Dictionary* (Nashville, TN: Holman Bible Publishers, 2003), 917.

[41] Charles W. Draper with Harrop Clayton, "Jewish Parties in the New Testament," ed. Chad Brand et al., *Holman Illustrated Bible Dictionary* (Nashville, TN: Holman Bible Publishers, 2003), 917.

religious leaders of his day. Jesus came to earth …

> **(1)** to bear witness to the truth to the Jewish people and by extension all who would read the Gospels (John 18:37),
>
> **(2)** to leave us an example, so that we might follow in his steps (1 Peter 2:21), and
>
> **(3)** He came not to be served but to serve, and to give his life as a ransom for many. (Matthew 20:28)

Anybody who has seriously studied Jesus knows that he was the greatest person that ever entered human history. Jesus Christ is the Son of God! He was the logos who entered the world to bring humanity the Word of God. No one has moved the hearts and minds of people like Jesus. No one turned the world upside down inside out like Jesus. No one has ever surpassed the life of Jesus and his impact upon the world. "Alexander the Great changed the language of the world, and Caesar changed the face of the world, but only Christ can change the heart of the world."[42] In 1926, James Allan Francis said these memorable words about Jesus. "Nineteen centuries have come and gone, and today Jesus is the central figure of the human race. And the leader of mankind's progress. All the armies that have ever marched; all the navies that have ever sailed; all the parliaments that have ever sat; all the kings that ever reigned put together have not affected the life of mankind on earth as powerfully as that one solitary life."[43] Notwithstanding, although considered controversial, radical, and revolutionary, we cannot deny the impact Jesus has had on mankind. His preaching and teaching did not fit into the sociopolitical religious context of which he

---

[42] T.T. Crabtree, The Zondervan Pastor's Annual An Idea and Resource Book, Zondervan Publishing House, 1995, 147.

[43] James Allan Francis, The Real Jesus and Other Sermons, Judson Press, 1926, p.121.

was born. For he was born poor, oppressed, and marginalized, and everything Jesus taught, preached, and did was an attack on this unjust context. Although his social context was unjust and oppressive, he never allowed himself to hate anybody. "Jesus rejected hatred. It was not because he lacked vitality or the strength. It was because he lacked the incentive. Jesus rejected hatred because he saw that hatred meant death to the mind, death to the spirit, death to communion with his Father. He affirmed life; and hatred was the great denial."[44] Anyone who chooses to follow Jesus must not allow hatred to rule in the heart and in the mind. The journey with Jesus is one of love, and this means tough love. It takes tough love to "Love your enemies and pray for those who persecute you." (Matthew 5:44) As difficult as this is; love is not an option but a mandate on the journey.

Because of the way he lived his life and sided with the poor and the hurting people in society, Jesus was not accepted by the religious and political power structure. They sought to destroy him because he would not go alone to get alone. He did not play the religious and political game. He would not keep quiet in the face of injustice and hypocrisy; he blew the whistle on corruption; he would not join the strong against the weak. He did not follow the social etiquette's of his times nor the religious strictness that prevented him for preaching the gospel to the poor, healing the brokenhearted, opening blinded eyes, setting the captives free, feeding the hungry, and preaching the acceptable year of the Lord. (Luke 4:18-19) Jesus was a man with purpose and he was very intentional about ushering in the Kingdom of God in the midst of an evil and corrupt world. Was he conservative or liberal? Was he right-winged or left-winged? Jesus was Kingdom winged, which means his approach was always coming from a Kingdom of God principle and

---

[44] Howard Thurman, Jesus and the Disinherited, Friends United Press, 1981, 88.

perspective. Jesus will never fit into our nicely packaged religious, social, and political categories. These man-made categories are limited, insufficient, and outright exclusive of others. They are carnal and non-spiritual at best. Jesus was of the Spirit of God, which supersedes all human categories.

Jesus was not waiting around to go to heaven but he brought heaven to human situations and circumstances. He was busy doing the work of the Kingdom of God, and his work and ministry put him at odds with the religious and political establishment of his day. Like the prophets before him who railed against injustice and unrighteousness, Jesus was truly an inconvenient leader. He preached an inconvenient gospel, taught an inconvenient truth, hung out with inconvenient people, started an inconvenient movement, demonstrated an inconvenient power and ushered in an inconvenient Kingdom. Because he was an inconvenient leader, he brought about a paradigm shift in the way we relate to God and one another. Because he would not compromise with evil, injustice, corruption, and hypocrisy, a conspiracy was launched to get rid of him. When people cannot control you, they will seek to destroy you. Jesus was an uncontrollable, politically incorrect, uncompromising leader who did not cow down to the rules and regulations of an oppressive political and religious establishment.

The religious leaders could not bring Jesus in line with their program so they made the decision to kill him. Jesus was causing too much conflict; his ministry was too much of a disruption to business as usual, and too inconvenient for many to follow. Many of his disciples walked off from him because what he asked of them was too hard and inconvenient. "So Jesus said to them, 'Truly, truly, I say to you, unless you eat the flesh of the Son of Man and drink his blood, you have no life in yourselves. He that feeds on my flesh and drinks my blood has eternal life, and I will raise him up on the last day. For my flesh is true food, and my blood is

35

true drink. Whoever feeds on my flesh and drinks my blood remains in me, and I in him.' ... When many of his disciples heard it, they said, "This is a hard saying; who can listen to it?" But Jesus, knowing in himself that his disciples were grumbling about this, said to them, 'Does this cause you to be offended?' ... After this, many of his disciples turned back and no longer walked with him." (John 6:54-66) They followed Jesus no more because what he asked of them was too hard, uncomfortable, and required too much sacrifice. They probably thought he was making a case for cannibalism. Had they continued on the journey with Jesus, they would have known that he was talking about eating his gospel and drinking of the Spirit of God. They did not know nor understand the life of the Spirit.

The Rich Young Ruler

Matthew 19:16-26 Updated American Standard Version (UASV)

[16] And look, a man came up to him, saying, "Teacher, what good deed must I do to have eternal life?" [17] And he said to him, "Why do you ask me about what is good? There is only one who is good. But if you want to enter into life, keep the commandments." [18] He said to him, "Which ones?" And Jesus said, "You shall not murder, You shall not commit adultery, You shall not steal, You shall not bear false witness; [19] Honor your father and mother, and, You shall love your neighbor as yourself."[45] [20] The young man said to him, "All these things I have kept; what am I still lacking?" [21] Jesus said to him: "If you want to be perfect,[46] go sell your belongings and give to the poor, and you will have treasure in heaven; and come be my follower." [22] But when the young

---

[45] A reference to Exodus 20:12-16; Leviticus 19:18; Deuteronomy 5:16-20

[46] Or *complete*

man heard this, he went away grieved, for he had many possessions.

²³ Then Jesus said to his disciples: "Truly I say to you that it will be difficult for a rich man to enter the Kingdom of the heavens. ²⁴ Again I say to you, it is easier for a camel to go through the eye of a needle than for a rich man to enter the Kingdom of God." ²⁵ When the disciples heard this, they were greatly astonished, saying, "Who then can be saved?" ²⁶ But Jesus looked at them and said, "With man this is impossible, but with God all things are possible."

The young man went away sorrowful because what Jesus asked of him was too hard and inconvenient. He admired Jesus but refused to follow Jesus. People are like this today. What Jesus asks of them is too hard and inconvenient, especially for many Christians. Many Christians today want a Christianity without Christ; a crown without a cross; triumph without trouble; church triumphant without church militancy. They do not want to sell out and give up everything to follow Jesus Christ. They don't want to sacrifice where it hurts; they don't want to stand up for it may cost them their reputation and life; they don't want to speak out for it may invite harm into their quiet lives. Many Christians want to live as convenient as they can. They want convenience over confronting the world with the Gospel of Jesus Christ. They want convenience over their convictions. Many hide in the crowd. They do not want responsibility; they do not want to be asked to do anything that may require time and sacrifice. For them, it is better to practice cultural Christianity than the Christianity of Christ. Cultural Christianity is politically correct Christianity. It is the private Christianity, which does not confront the evils and injustice of society; it is the Christianity that makes no spiritual and morals demands, and the Christianity that "Strain at a gnat, and swallow a camel," which means they major in the minor and minor in the major. Cultural Christianity does not want to disturb the status quo. It wants to go alone to get alone. Jesus warns against this kind of lukewarm Christianity. "Not everyone who says to me, 'Lord, Lord,' will enter the kingdom of heaven, but the one who does the will of my Father who is in heaven." (Matthew 7:21) Our question here is, 'What is the will of the Father?' It is all of those things that the Word of God, i.e., the Father says that we are supposed to be doing or not doing. The apostle John wrote something very similar to Jesus' words above in his first letter.

Do Not Love the World

1 John 2:15-17 Updated American Standard Version (UASV)

15 Do not love the world or the things in the world. If anyone loves the world, the love of the Father is not in him. **16** For all that is in the world, the lust of the flesh and the lust of the eyes and the boastful pride of life, is not from the Father, but is from the world. **17** The world is passing away, and its lusts; but the one who does the will of God remains forever.

Notice how it shows us a thing that we **are not** to be doing. Now, we should have a follow-up question, 'what does it mean to be no part of the world?' It is not what I think, feel, or believe, or what you feel, think, or believe it means. It is what John meant by his words. He tells some of what he meant here in verse 16, "the lust of the flesh and the lust of the eyes and the boastful pride of life." Now, more questions are in order, 'what did John mean by the lust of the flesh?' What did he mean by the lust of the eyes'? 'How can our eyes lust?' Lastly, 'What is the boastful pride of life mean?' We get at the answers by digging into word study dictionaries, commentaries, Bible dictionaries, and Bible cyclopedias. Why should we study the deeper things of God's Word? Dr. Lee M. Fields answers that for us, "'Deep' study is no guarantee that mature faith will result, but shallow study guarantees that immaturity continues." (Fields 2008, xiii) We have addressed an example of thing that we **are not to do**, let us consider **a few things that we are to do**. "So Jesus said to the Jews who had believed him, 'If you remain in my word, you are truly my disciples, and you will know the truth, and the truth will set you free.'" (John 8:31-32) What did Jesus mean our 'remaining in his word'? Jesus said, "By this all men will know that you are my disciples, if you have love for one another." (John 13:35) What does it really mean to have love for one another? Jesus said, "My Father is glorified by this: that you bear much fruit, and prove to be my disciples." (John 15:8) What does it mean to bear much fruit? Finding out the will of the Father is not just what Jesus says, but what all 40+ Bible authors under inspiration said that we **are to do** and **not do** that evidence whether we are doing the will of the Father; otherwise we will hear Jesus' words, 'I never knew you; depart from me, you who practice lawlessness.' (Matthew 7:23) From this alone, we can see that it is highly important that we accurately understand what the will of the Father is and is not. It certainly is not us reading our will into the Scriptures. It is what those 40+ Bible authors meant by the words that they used. In the end, this means that we need to understand how to interpret the Scriptures correctly; to get out of it what the author meant, and not read into it what we think the author meant.[47]

Many Christians across denominational and racial lines want a convenient religion. They want ease and comfort. They can clearly see that "The harvest is plentiful but the

---

[47] INTERPRETING THE BIBLE: Introduction to Biblical Hermeneutics by Edward D. Andrews
http://www.christianpublishers.org/apps/webstore/products/show/7044598
A Basic Guide to Interpreting the Bible: Playing by the Rules by Robert H. Stein
https://www.amazon.com/Basic-Guide-Interpreting-Bible-Playing/dp/080103373X/
Basic Bible Interpretation by Roy B. Zuck
https://www.amazon.com/Basic-Bible-Interpretation-Roy-Zuck/dp/0781438772

labors are few," but they want convenience. They can see the needs of their church and community, but they want convenience. They can see the need for evangelism, but they want convenience. They can see the need of families and children, but they want convenience. They can see how greed, racism, and the oppression of the poor are putting the nation on the edge of moral collapse, but they want convenience. Too many Bible carrying, noisemaking, Sunday attending Christians fail to involve themselves in the work of the Kingdom of God. It is too risky, too demanding, and too outright inconvenient. The religious leaders during the times of Jesus were too much concerned about their titles, power, and influence to join Jesus in the work of the Kingdom of God. These leaders against Jesus were too afraid to take risks, too afraid to think outside the box, too afraid to speak truth to power, and too afraid to join the revolutionary movement against wrong, evil, and injustice. These coward and unconverted leaders launched an unholy conspiracy against Jesus and finally influenced the people to join them in saying, "Crucify him, crucify him, crucify him." They knew unless they kill Jesus they could no longer exploit and take advantage of an uninformed people. Jesus was awakening people to the detriment of their religious and political leaders.

The religious leaders wanted him crucified because his presence was inconvenient; his preaching was inconvenient; his teaching was inconvenient; his Kingdom of God talk was inconvenient. His healing power was inconvenient; his love, his mercy, and his compassion were too inconvenient for them so they cried with a loud voice, "Crucify him, crucify him, crucify him." The religious leaders and the misguided people wanted Jesus crucified because he didn't go around with the same fear and weakness they had in themselves, and this made Jesus an inconvenient leader and preacher. Not much has changed today. When people cannot get you to join them in their foolish and unjust cause, you are an inconvenience to them; and they will treat you with the same contempt as they did with Jesus. People who have decided to follow Jesus Christ must be prepared to hear the same words in one way or another, "Crucify him, crucify him." He is a rebel; "Crucify him;" he is a conscientious objector, "Crucify him;" he doesn't go alone to get alone, "Crucify him; he is a loose cannon," Crucify him;" these followers of Jesus are brained washed, "Crucify them;" they are too loud in praise and worship, Crucify them." People who are following Jesus must understand that "The servant is no greater than his master." (John 15:20) They thought Christ was inconvenient and they will also think his followers are inconvenient.

Inconvenience is a word we don't like to hear, but if you are going to follow Jesus Christ and advance the Kingdom of God, then you must embrace inconvenience. You must practice a disruptive spirituality that disrupts wrong, evil, and injustice. It is much, much, much, easier doing things the convenient way, following the path of least resistance, but Jesus didn't call us to a convenient way of life. He calls us to take up our cross and follow him. It is the convenient thing to follow the crowd, and go alone to get alone, but Jesus said, "Follow me." It's convenient making money and acquiring status and prestige, but Jesus said, "But be you seeking[48] the kingdom of God and his righteousness, and all these things will be added to you." (Matthew 6:33) It is convenient to be resentful and unforgiving, but Jesus said, "For if you forgive not [others] for their trespasses, neither will your Father forgive your trespasses." It is convenient to love your family, love your neighbors, and love your friends, but Jesus wants us to be inconvenient and love the loveless, love those who don't live like us, think like us, look like us, speak like us, and believe like us. This covers all people. To follow Jesus Christ you must prepare to do all of the

---

[48] Gr., *zeteite*; the verb form indicates continuous action.

inconvenient things you may not feel like doing on this journey. We are commanded to love when we want to hate. We are commanded to forgive when we want to hold grudges. We are commanded to seek first the Kingdom of God and his righteousness when we want to seek our own way of life and comfort. As difficult as it is, these things and more are required on this journey.

Jesus is calling his followers to understand that this faith journey is not about us. It is not about our will and our way. It is not about what makes us look good; what makes us prosperous and successful. Too often we lace Jesus around our neatly package ideas that promote us, our ideas, and our religious and political philosophy. We cast him in so many different ways that we have constructed a Jesus that looks like us, talks like us, and thinks like us. We have customized Jesus to our liking. "But Jesus is not customizable. He has not left himself open to interpretation, adaptation, innovation, or alteration. He has revealed himself clearly through his Word, and we have no right to personalize him. Instead, he revolutionizes us. As we follow Jesus, we believe Jesus, even when his Word confronts (and often contradicts) the deeply held assumptions, beliefs, and convictions of our lives, our families, our friends, our culture, and sometimes even our churches."[49] Following Jesus is not about us but for us to enter the Kingdom of God to enjoy eternal life with God through Jesus Christ.

As stated earlier, this inconvenient journey is not easy because it entails following an inconvenient Savior, practice an inconvenient love, draw inspiration from an inconvenient Bible; teach an inconvenient ethics; preach an inconvenient gospel; filled with an inconvenient Spirit; live an inconvenient lifestyle; being an inconvenient servant to others; sing inconvenient songs, and pray some inconvenient prayers.

---

[49] David Platt, What Did Jesus Really Mean When He Said Follow Me, Tyndale House Publisher, 2013, 26.

And one of these days, die an inconvenient death, go home to an inconvenient heaven, and live forever with an inconvenient God through an inconvenient Savior, Jesus Christ. Please understand to surrender all and follow Jesus Christ is an inconvenience. It means you will have to go across some rough terrain; walk through some deep waters; go through some tough circumstances, thrown into lion den situations; labeled awful names, misunderstood, persecuted, and may be put to death. The journey is not admirable. Kierkegaard said, "In His actual life there was absolutely nothing to admire . . . unless one would admire poverty, wretchedness, the suffering of contempt. He did not even escape the last degradation, that of being pitied, of being a pitiable object of commiseration. No, there verily was not the least thing to admire."[50]

From a world's perspective, there was nothing to admire about Jesus, prepare yourself because there will be nothing to admire about you as a follower! In this world of oppression, corruption, and injustice, there is nothing to admire about you when you decide to change reality from what is to what ought to be. What you will stand for or against will not be admired. The sacrifices you make for the Kingdom of God will not be admired. The light you allow to shine in the darkness will not be admired. The love you demonstrate to others won't be admired. Anything you do to lift up Jesus and his cross in this world won't be admired. The same contempt the world held against Jesus will also be held against you. But, be of good cheer because what you do for Christ will not be in vain. There is a hymn that you should remember while on this dangerous journey:

> I have decided to follow Jesus,
> I have decided to follow Jesus,
> I have decided to follow Jesus,
> No turning back, no turning back!

---

[50] Soren Kierkegaard, Training in Christianity, 234.

Though no one join me, still I will follow,
Though no one join me, still I will follow,
Though no one join me, still I will follow,
No turning back, no turning back!
The world behind me, the cross before me,
The world behind me, the cross before me,
The world behind me, the cross before me,
No turning back, no turning back![51]

Now, if you feel what you have read so far about following Jesus Christ is too much of an inconvenience, stop reading now because the following chapters will only get worse before it gets better.

---

[51] Norman Johnson, "I Have Decided to Follow Jesus" copyright 1963.

CHAPTER TWO Expect Temptation

Temptation coaxes us toward sin, and sin leads to sickness and death, and ultimately confinement in the realm of the evil one.—Frederica Mathewes-Green

When you decide to follow Jesus Christ inevitably you will run into some kind of temptation. Temptation comes in many forms, shapes, and sizes; it is designed to thwart your walk with Christ and render you ineffective for the Kingdom of God. It comes to draw the heart and mind away from obedience to God. It is not accidental; it is intentional. The intent is to get you to act and live contrary to what God through Jesus Christ has commanded you to do. It comes to get you to compete with God rather than cooperate with God. It is to get you to turn away from obedience to rebellion against God. John Owen says, "Temptation is like a knife, that may either cut the meat or the throat of a man; it may be his food or his poison, his exercise or his destruction."[52] It comes to sever the relationship between Jesus Christ and his followers. For this reason, Jesus said, "Keep on the watch and pray continually, so that you may not enter into temptation. The spirit, of course, is eager, but the flesh is weak." (Matthew 26:41) A follower must watch and see temptation coming and prepare through prayer how to overcome it. Temptation may come at your extreme weakest point or your extreme highest point. Whenever you are at your highest or lowest point, make sure your guard is not down because this is when temptation hits you the hardest. Some of the greatest men and women of the Judeo-Christian faith have been tempted, and a few had their guard down and they fall into temptation that caused them trouble later. For example Samson, David, and Solomon had their

---

[52] John Owens, Overcoming Sin & Temptation, Edited by Kelly M. Kapic and Justin Taylor, Crossway Books, 2006, 152.

guard down and yielded to temptation, and it caused them pain and grief later. Others like Joseph and Job did not yield, and they were extremely blessed long after the temptation. The point is on this Christian journey you will be tempted.

"Temptation is a fact of life for all of us, Christians as much as unbelievers. The difference is that if you are a son of God, you have supernatural power available to you to say no to temptation and live a life that pleases our Creator."[53] Others make excuses about yielding to temptation, but as a follower of Jesus Christ, you have the power not to give in to temptation. Money, fame, fortune, position and power are forms of temptation that are waved before you to get you to yield to the tricks and trade of the temper. "The man who goes around thinking that temptation is no problem may be right, because he has probably been conquered by it so often and surrendered to it so consistently that he no longer feels any conflict. Paul knew he would struggle with sin as long as he was in the flesh."[54] Therefore, never underestimate the power of temptation. Keep in mind as Larry Dixon said, "There's an enemy out there, waiting to bring us down. Actually, 'out there' doesn't really describe its location. It's a traitor in our midst, posing as an ally as it deceives and attacks us, opposing all that is good. It promises what it cannot deliver; it knows our weaknesses and shows us no mercy. We cannot fight this enemy on our own. It will drag us down to defeat and despair unless we recognize it and are equipped to oppose."[55] Satan, the tempter is far superior in knowledge, and he wants you to disobey God and lose your position and possession as he lost his. Satan is busy trying to tempt you out of your eternal blessing. If the tempter can get you to yield to the temptation, it frustrates God's plan for

---

[53] Tony Evans, No More Excuses Be The Man God Made You To Be, CrossWay Books, 1996, 134.

[54] Ibid., 137.

[55] Larry Dixon, When Temptation Strikes, Published by CLC Publications, 2008, 19.

your life and causes spiritual, emotional, and psychological damage to you, your marriage, family, church, community, and other connected relationships. Your yielding to temptation is sin and it does affect others. Never think that yielding to temptation does not affect others.

For example, when Adam and Eve yielded to temptation and sinned, it affected the whole human race. Humanity has been struggling against sin and its devastating effects ever since. When "Satan rose up against Israel and incited David to take a census of Israel (1 Chronicles 21:1), David yield to the temptation, and because of his sin, seventy thousand men lost their lives. Temptation comes to wreck your relationship with God and one another:

> Temptation, then in general, is anything, state, way, or condition that, upon any account whatsoever, has a force or efficacy to seduce, to draw the mind and heart of a [person] from its obedience, which God requires of him, into any sin, in any degree of it whatsoever. In particular, that is a temptation to any man which causes or occasions him to sin, or in anything to go off from his duty, either by bringing evil into his heart, or drawing out that evil that is in his heart, or any other way diverting him from communion with God and that constant, equal, universal obedience, in matter and manner, that is required of him.[56]

It goes without saying that every follower of Jesus Christ must be prepared to struggle with temptation. A follower must wrestle with temptation every day on the Christian journey. Ungodly forces are going to come at you to do or act in ways that would call into question the authenticity of your Christian walk. Do not take these ungodly forces for granted because they are strong, cunning, and very

---

[56] John Owens, Overcoming Sin and Temptation, 156.

manipulative. They have money, position, and power to persuade you. They come as angels of light but beware they are full of deceit and deadly poison. If they can get you to buy into the ungodly schemes of this world, and denounce the just way, the righteous way, and the godly way, they can keep you from doing the will of God on earth as it is in heaven. They can take over your flesh and cause you to live a life in rebellion against God. You must understand that "For the desires of the flesh are against the Spirit, and the desires of the Spirit are against the flesh, for these are opposed to each other, so that you may not do the things you want to do." (Galatians 5:17) For this reason, it is mandatory to "watch and pray" because of Satan, the tempter is determined to draw you into sin and then accuse you before the throne of God. The tempter knows that sin separates you from God, and through separation, the tempter and demons of hell will try to destroy you.

Russell D. Moore reminds us how angry these malevolent spirits are in the universe. "Jesus, like the prophets before him, showed us that the cosmic order was hijacked millennia ago by these "rulers" and "authorities" (Ephesians 6:12). Jesus in his taking on our nature, offering himself up in death as a sacrifice for our sins, and turning back the curse of death in his resurrection, has ended the claim these demonic powers have on the universe. These powers don't want to give up their dark reign, so they are lashing back, and with fury. This means war. The sheer animal force of temptation ought to remind us of something: the universe is demon-haunted. It also ought to remind us there's only one among us who has ever wrestled the demons and prevailed."[57] Jesus took on our flesh, and he defeated Satan, the tempter. The tempter no longer has power over your flesh because Jesus Christ broke this hold on humanity by shedding his blood. Dietrich

---

[57] Russell D. Moore, Tempted and Tried: Temptation and the Triumph of Christ, Crossway Publisher, Wheaton, Illinois, 2011, 20.

Bonhoeffer said, "The temptation of Christ was harder, unspeakably harder than the temptation of Adam; for Adam carried nothing in himself which could have given the temper a claim and power over him. But Christ bore in himself the whole burden of the flesh, under the curse, under condemnation; and yet his temptation was henceforth to bring help and salvation to all flesh."[58]

Furthermore, the Spirit that was in Christ is also in his followers, which means you can wrestle and overcome these demon spirits as Jesus did. "We overcome temptation the same way he did, by trusting in our Father and hearing his voice. The danger we face presently is not cognitive but primal. The demons are thinkers. They know who God is, and they tremble before that truth. (James 2:19) Mere intellect cannot ensure that we are "led not into temptation" or "delivered from evil." Only "faith working through love" (Galatians 5:6) can do that."[59] Therefore, prepare yourself in prayer and the meditation of God's word because every day Satan, the chief demon, will tempt you in one way or another to disobey the Gospel of Jesus Christ. This is always the goal to temptation to get followers of Jesus Christ to become fans or admirers by asserting their will and way above God's will. The tempter knows once followers decide to follow their own way, their own wisdom, and knowledge; they can easily be fooled into thinking they are on the narrow path when they have actually merged onto the broad way that leads to death, hell, and destruction.

"The devil [i.e., the tempter] took him [Jesus] to a very high mountain and showed him all the kingdoms of the world and their glory." (Matthew 4:8) All the riches and glory of this world was shown to Jesus to get him to come

---

[58] Dietrich Bonhoeffer, Creation And Fall Temptation Two Biblical Studies, Simon & Schuster Publisher, 1959, 117.

[59] Russell D. Moore, Tempted and Tried: Temptation and the Triumph of Christ, 22-23.

under the authority of the temper. Jesus knew his purpose; and he knew that the tempter caused the first Adam to bring sin into the world, and had Jesus yield to the temptation, the power, and authority that the tempter had over humanity would have never been broken. You must remember that you are a servant to whom you obey. Adam and Eve became servants of the devil, and the tempter wanted Jesus to obey and become a servant as well. However, Jesus did not yield to the temptation, and you must not yield to it regardless of how delicious and attractive it appears. Jesus did not give up his Father's authority over his life to come under the tempter's authority. Howard Thurman said, "It was because Jesus was not willing to give up the initiative over his own life, even for a chance to get his hands on enough power that conceivably could alter the arrangement of affairs that they killed him. And he discovered that for a man who is willing to hold initiative over his own life under God, even death is a little thing. Somehow he can stand whatever life does to him."[60]

Therefore, you must remember that when the tempter cannot get you to yield, he will return with another temptation more delicious and attractive than the temptation before. In the tempter's arsenal is the transformative power to deceive. The devil can change himself into an angel of light (2 Corinthians 11:14), and if you are not rooted as a follower of Jesus Christ, the tempter may cause you to think what he is presenting to you is a blessing from God when it is really an entrapment from the tempter. Don't underestimate the slickness of the tempter. He may start with something small to whet your appetite, and then overtime set you up to be entrapped into something big to the point that you are now a slave of sin. This is the reason nations are at war with one another; they have become slaves of sin. Once you are a

---

[60] Howard Thurman, Temptations of Jesus, Friends United Press, Richmond, Indiana, 1978, 43.

slave of sin, you cannot be a follower of Jesus Christ. When this happens, the tempter's mission is accomplished because admirers or fans will do their own will and not the will of God.

Therefore, do not take lightly how yielding to temptation can ruin you, your family, your business, and your relationships with others. A follower must always keep his and her eyes and mind on Jesus Christ or otherwise you can start sinking into the water of temptation. With the kind of world we live in, it is getting harder and harder not to yield to temptation. In this entertaining, instant gratification, and sexually charged culture, temptation is all around us. It is at our fingertips for you to bite the bait and fall into sin. Temptation is a trap, a snare, a stumbling block along each step of the Christian journey. Some describe it as a "folk in like's road way." Others see it as a constant pull, an allurement into the dark, shady, and immoral ways of life. A follower of Jesus Christ must "Be alert and of sober mind. Your enemy the devil prowls around like a roaring lion looking for someone to devour (Peter 5:8)." Satan, the temper knows your weakness; he knows your thoughts and imagination. He is also spirit cable of getting into your thought processes and wielding in your mind all the desires of the flesh. He wants you to think that disobeying God is not a big deal; it is not that serious. In fact, he will convey to you that you are human, and that God understands as a human you will try certain things. Once you try drugs, sex, adultery, fornication, alcohol, and those things that the Holy Spirit tugs at you not to do, the temper will convince you it is ok not that serious. Maybe the first, second, and third time you tried something the temper convinced you were not a big deal, but after a while you find yourself hooked, addicted, and fighting the demons of hell. Once you yield to temptation, it becomes easier and easier to sin over and over again.

Therefore, the temper will not tempt you with orange juice if he knows you love chocolate milk. The tempter has studied your desires and understood your appetite. Therefore, when he tempts you understand he is aware of your strengths and weaknesses. It is up to you not to allow the tempter to take advantage of your most vulnerable area of weakness. The tempter cannot make you do anything. He can bring the thought, the idea, and suggestion to you but he cannot force you to yield to the temptation. Yielding or not yielding is within your power. Too many people say, "The devil made me do it." No, the devil did not make you do it; he brought it to you, and you did not resist it. The Scripture teaches, "Resist[61] the devil, and he will flee from you." (James 4:7) You have the power to resist the temptation, and with the Spirit of the Lord in you, "No temptation has overtaken you but such as is common to man; and God is faithful, who will not allow you to be tempted beyond what you are able, but with the temptation will provide the way of escape also, so that you will be able to endure it." (1 Corinthians 10:13) Understand, you can overcome temptation; you don't have to yield. As there is a way into temptation, there is a way out of temptation. Never believe you have to yield to temptation just because you are human. Jesus was also human, and as Howard Thurman stated, "I am so very glad that he struggled and triumphed. And so he speaks to me all the time that I might struggle, if, happily, I too might triumph."[62] You have the power to overcome temptation, but you cannot do this alone. You must have Jesus Christ on the inside of you to overcome temptation. Always remember, "The one who is in you is greater than the one who is in the world." (1 John 4:4) With the Holy Spirit guiding you through your understanding and applying the Word of God correctly, temptation has no power over you. Never forget that "The temptations of our Lord are the temptations of his church. The church as the people of God must be committed to 'the food that abides.'

---

[61] I.e., *Stand against*

[62] Ibid., 31.

It must use power, but it had better be the power of the gospel. The church must pray 'not my will but thy will be done.' The temptations of our Lord are repeated in the temptations that come to you in your daily vocation and calling as public figures and private persons in the Kingdom of God."[63]

Therefore, remember when you are doing God's will, the tempter will try to tempt you out of it. Try to live right and see won't the tempter try to stop you. Try to build the Kingdom of God and see won't the tempter try to tear it down. Try to do justly, love mercy, and walk humbly with God, see won't the tempter make sure stumbling blocks are thrown in your way. Try to live as a Christian ought and teach as the Master taught and see won't the hounds of hell pursue your footsteps. Preach the gospel without any sweetener and see won't people get offended. "But none of these are new temptations. The temptations themselves are, as the Scripture puts it, 'common to man' (1 Cor. 10:13), and in Jesus' desert testing we see how true this is. Here the Scriptures identify for us the universal strategies of temptation. You will be tempted exactly as Jesus was because Jesus was being tempted exactly as we are. You will be tempted with consumption, security, and status. You will be tempted to provide for yourself, to protect yourself, and to exalt yourself."[64] However, when you desire to advance spiritually and understand that you are your brothers and sisters keepers, see won't Satan, the tempter try to tempt you out of it! All kinds of tricks and temptations come to deter you from the course God through Christ is calling you to. The tempter doesn't want the gospel of Jesus Christ to go forward. He doesn't want followers to carry out the agenda

---

[63] Walter F. Wolbrecht, "The Temptations of Christ, The Church, and The Christian" Augsburg Sermons Series C, 1973, Augsburg Publishing House, 91.

[64] Russell D. Moore, Tempted and Tried: Temptation and the Triumph of Christ, 20.

of the Kingdom of God. However, regardless of his temptations, you have the power to tell Satan as Jesus said to him, "Get behind me, Satan! You are a stumbling block to me; for you are not setting your mind on the things of God, but on the things of man." (Matthew 16:23) Never forget that you have the power to order Satan to get behind you! The following hymn can help you through your temptation as you journey with Jesus Christ:

Yield not to temptation, For yielding is sin;
Each victory will help you, Some other to win;
Fight valiantly onward, Evil passions subdue;
Look ever to Jesus, He will carry you through.
Ask the Savior to help you, Comfort, strength and keep you;
He is willing to aid you, He will carry you through.
Shun evil companions, Bad language disdain;
God's name hold in reverence, Nor take it in vain;
Be thoughtful and earnest, Kind hearted and true
Look ever to Jesus, He will carry you through.
Ask the Savior to help you, Comfort, strengthen and keep you;
He is willing to aid you, He will carry you through.
To him that over cometh, God giveth a crown;
Through faith we will conquer, Though often cast down;
He who is our Savior, Our strength will renew;
Look ever to Jesus, He will carry you through,
Ask the Savior to help you, Comfort, strengthen and keep you;
He is willing to aid you, He will carry you through.[65]

---

[65] Horatio R. Palmer, Yield Not, 1834-1907, from Songs of Praise, 1992.

CHAPTER THREE Expect Rejection

Isaiah 53:3 Updated American Standard Version (UASV)

³ He was despised and rejected[66] by men;
   a man of pains,[67] and acquainted with grief;[68]
and as one from whom men hide their faces
   he was despised, and we esteemed him not.

Rejection can be one of the most devastating and psychologically disturbing experiences a person can go through. No one likes rejection. No one likes to feel that their family, friends, church, peers, and society have rejected them. Rejection hurts deeply; it wounds severely; and it can emotionally tear a person apart. Rejection comes in many forms. People are rejected because of their skin color, because they are tall or short, thin or obese, young or old, educated or uneducated, zip codes, and a variety of reasons and assumptions. We hear story after story about hazing, initiations, college and university pledges, and other acts people do just to be accepted. Some people do almost anything and allow almost anything done to them just to be accepted. Acceptance into certain groups, clubs, organizations, schools, and companies is like vitamin A to the ego. People have a sense of belonging; a sense of pride, a sense of accomplishment, a sense of self-esteem, a sense of importance, and a sense of power and privilege when others have accepted them. There is nothing inherently wrong with acceptance by others because humans are social beings; and no person, group or community likes it when they have been rejected. Some revolutions are the results of social and economic rejection. Rejection is the worst of emotional

---

[66] Deliberately *forsaken*; *abandoned*; *avoided* by others.

[67] One who knows and understands suffering by experience.

[68] One who is familiar with sickness and grief.

wounds. Many people fear the pain of rejection, and this is the reason they go alone with wrong, evil, and injustice. This is the reason they refuse to stand up and speak up during times they really need to. They keep their feelings and opinions to themselves because the fear and pain of rejection can be too much to bear.

Guy Winch says that our fear and pain of rejection can be traced to our past. "Humans are social animals; being rejected from our tribe or social group in our pre-civilized past would have meant losing access to food, protection, and mating partners, making it extremely difficult to survive. Being ostracized would have been akin to receiving a death sentence. Because the consequences of ostracism were so extreme, our brains developed an early-warning system to alert us when we were at risk for being "voted off the island" by triggering sharp pain whenever we experienced even a hint of social rejection."[69] Therefore, people work hard to be accepted. Studies show that many high achievers have been rejected as a child in one way or another, and they practically work themselves overtime to prove to others that they have worth. Rejection for some people has been a springboard for achievement. They cannot accept the fact that they are not good enough, smart enough, good looking enough and don't measure up. So, they work hard to prove to themselves and others their intrinsic worth as a human being. They spend a lifetime achieving because of the fear and pain of rejection.

Now, there is nothing wrong with achieving as a result of intrinsic worth. We all have intrinsic worth given to us by the Creator. Paul said, "But we have this treasure in earthen vessels,[70] so that the surpassing power may be of God and not to us." (2 Corinthians 4:7) God's Spirit guiding us is the treasure that gives us worth, and everybody needs to know

---

[69] Guy Winch, Emotional First Aid, Hudson Street Press, 2013, 24.

[70] Or *in jars of clay*

that he or she has this treasure. However, what people do not understand is that even if they do not win the approval of others they still have self-worth because it is a gift of God. Rejection does not remove this gift in us. Working hard to prove we have this gift is not necessary. Human achievement is the result of the gift of God. However, it is understandable how rejection can cause people to question their self-worth. Many kids who have been in foster homes question their self-worth because they cannot understand why their biological parents rejected them. Many foster kids develop mental and behavioral problems as a result of feeling rejected. When people do not feel loved and are ostracized, rejection can scar so deep that many people develop psychological and social problems. Some become self-destructive and social psychopaths. They kill and turn on others out of their pain of rejection. We should never underestimate the traumatic pain of rejection. Rejection can really turn people's lives upside down; it is just that powerful. "When our need to belong remains unsatisfied for extended periods of time, either because of the rejections we've experienced or because we lack opportunities to create supportive relationships, it can have a powerful and detrimental effect on our physical and psychological health."[71]

Now, as bad and traumatizing as rejection is, once you decide to follow Jesus Christ, you will experience a new kind of rejection on the journey. This rejection may come within your home, in your marriage, in your workplace, among friends, and even in the church. When rejection comes, understand that it is not personal. There is nothing deficient about you and your self-worth. This rejection is spiritual. It is the result of following Jesus Christ who is in you and at work transforming people and culture for the Kingdom of God. Since change doesn't come easy, especially if this change puts people at some kind of social and economic disadvantage,

---

[71] Ibid., 38.

people will reject you. Jesus said, "A servant is not greater than his master." (John 13:16) What is done to the Master is also done to the servant. Those who follow Jesus Christ will be rejected as the Master was rejected. "Not only Jews but also Greeks and Romans, medievalists and moderns, Westerners and Orientals have rejected Christ because they saw in him a threat to their culture."[72] Since you are a follower of Christ, people will reject you to because you are a threat to the culture around you as well. You may be called all kinds of names and all kinds of labels may be attached to you. Don't take it personal. It is the Christ in you.

For example, the scribes, the priest, and the Pharisees rejected Jesus because he was bringing about change in their nicely knit religious culture of which the Mosaic Law was so strict people were heavy burdened. Jesus rallied against this strictness, and they rejected him because he would not go alone with the status quo. When Jesus came to Nazareth, the hometown where he was raised, he went into the temple, read from Isaiah, and told the hearers that this Scripture is fulfilled in their hearing. The people became hostile to the point that they took him to throw him headlong over the cliff on which the city was built. (Luke 4:17-29) Another example of rejection is when Jesus delivered a demon possessed man to his right mind, and the people in the town of Gadara ask Jesus to leave. Can you imagine asking the Savior to leave who came to give life and give more abundantly to leave? The Gadarenes thought more of ham than human life. (Luke 8:27-37) These are just two examples of the many rejections Jesus experienced during his ministry. In spite of his mighty work among the people, the Jewish religious leaders did not want to accept Jesus as the Messiah. They resented Jesus' fame and were envious of his miracles. Jesus reminds his followers that, "A prophet is not without

---

[72] H. Richard Niebuhr, Christ and Culture, Harper & Row, Publishers, 1951, 4.

honor, except in his hometown and among his relatives and in his own household." (Mark 6:4) Followers of Jesus Christ must adjust to rejection. Yes, it is painful. Yes, it is wounding. Yes, it is unsettling. But, understand it comes with the territory as a follower of Jesus Christ. Jesus, said, "You will be hated by all because of my name, but it is the one who has endured to the end who will be saved." (Matthew 10:22) Followers of Christ must prepare for rejection and not take it personally because we are in a spiritual warfare.

During the early Christian movement, followers of Jesus were being rejected everywhere. They were thrown out of cities, thrown out of homes; and thrown out of synagogues. Many were thrown to hungry lions; others were dipped in hot oil; some had their heads cut off for following Jesus whom they believed was the Son of God. As it was mentioned earlier, enemies of Jesus are not only on the outside but also on the inside of the church. Stephen who was a leader in the church believed in Jesus and made his stance concerning his faith. Just because he attacked the causes of evil and oppression as Jesus had done, the people inside the church rejected his message and stoned him to death. Stephen is believed to be the first Christian martyr who was willing to pay the price for his faith in Jesus Christ. Over the centuries, Christians have been rejected for advancing a gospel that does not set well with the powers that be and the gatekeepers for those in power.

In European history, the Catholic Church rejected the protestant reformation of the 16th century because its leaders thought this change would put the church at an economic and social disadvantage. Martin Luther's 95 theses that were nailed on the door of the church at Whittenburg was an act to reform the church but the leaders of church rejected him. In addition, years later during the abolitionist movement of the 19th century, the abolitionists were hated and rejected in the south because they were pushing for a change that the south believed would put them at an economic disadvantage.

The south rejected the moral suasion of the truth that slavery is morally wrong and it resulted in a civil war of which tens of thousands were killed. Martin Luther King Jr. and the civil rights movement met with fierce rejection. Many within the Christian church rejected this movement saying it stirs up trouble. Those who follow Jesus Christ are thought of as troublemakers because wherever there is wrong, evil, and injustice, they cannot be silent onlookers. Followers must understand it is their duty to correct these situations because the Kingdom of God does not cooperate with evil and injustice. It does not cooperate with racism and oppression of any people. These and other examples show the rejection you must prepare for when following Jesus Christ and the redemptive work of the Kingdom of God.

Wherever Jesus leads you, especially in the transformation work of unjust and inhumane situations, don't be surprised when you encounter rejection. Don't be surprised if those in your church and your circle of influence exhibit a cold shoulder toward you. Don't be surprised when you are denied a job, overlooked for a promotion, refused a pay raise, and not invited to certain functions and places. These are, and there are many more forms of rejection that will cost you for being a follower and not just an admirer of Jesus Christ. The reason for a lot of rejection, especially in the church, is there are more admirers than followers of Jesus Christ. The Danish theologian Soren Kierkegaard made a very cogent observation of the difference between an admirer and a follower of Jesus Christ:

> A follower is or strives to be what he admires. An admirer holds himself personally aloof, consciously or unconsciously, he does not discern that the object of his admiration makes a claim upon him to be or strive to be the thing he admires. . . . For when no danger is present, when there is a dead calm, when everything is favorable to Christianity, it is only too easy to mistake an admirer for a follower,

and this may pass quite unobserved, the admirer may die in the illusion that the relationship he assumed was the true one. Attention therefore to contemporaneousness (the call of discipleship)! . . . . And at the beginning of His life Christ had many, many admirers. Admiration was eager to spread its web for Him also, hoping to appropriate Him. . . . And when the time came to make the reckoning, it resulted finally that among the one-time admiring contemporaries there were found barely twelve followers of whom one was only an admirer, or as he is generally called, a traitor, namely, Judas, who precisely because he was an admirer quite naturally became a traitor. . . . The admirer is only effeminately or selfishly in love with greatness; if trouble comes or danger, he draws back; and if this is not possible, he becomes a traitor, as a way of liberating himself from the one time object of his admiration.[73]

Understand then that as you demonstrate discipleship, your circle of friends may become few because the world and many Christians are admirers, not disciples. Your rejection is the direct result of being a disciple. When you take serious the call to follow Jesus as a disciple, Satan, the devil gets angry and aggravated and launches an attack against you to prevent any influence you can have in getting others to follow Jesus. So, don't be surprised when rejection comes from places that you believe should be your greatest support. Admirers of Christ are everywhere clothed in the garments of being disciples, and if you are not aware that many in your circle may be admirers, not disciples, you may be tempted to turn back from following Christ or join the crowd of

---

[73] Soren Kierkegaard, Training in Christianity, Translated, with an introduction and notes, by Walter Lowrie, Princeton University Press, 1972, 234, 239.

admirers, which will greatly impact your effectiveness and put your soul in jeopardy before the judgment seat of Christ.

Jesus Christ is not calling for admirers. He made this very clear while he was on earth. If he was calling for admirers, he never would have disturbed the religious and political order of his day. He would have never turned over the tables of the money changers. He would have never disturbed people's conscience and attacked their complacency. He would have never kept religious leaders angry, cut off profits of morticians by raising up the dead, put ophthalmologists out of business by giving sight to the blind, practiced civil disobedience, break injunctions, eat with social outcasts, bless children, befriend prostitutes and tax collectors, forgive sins, and give fresh courage to the poor, the oppressed and the downtrodden. These acts of love made Jesus an enemy to the political and religious establishment. Had Jesus been seeking admirers, he would have never taught and preached a revolutionary gospel, offered a Kingdom diametrically opposite of the Kingdom of this world, and done anything that would bring down the disdainment of the religious and political leaders. No, Jesus was not calling for admirers.

People who experienced the miracles of Jesus followed after him, but when Jesus told them "He that feeds on my flesh and drinks my blood has eternal life, and I will raise him up on the last day. After this, many of his disciples turned back and no longer walked with him. (John 6:54, 66) They rejected him. People were willing to be admirers, not followers. The rich young ruler who came to Jesus inquiring about eternal life and Jesus told him to sell all his goods and give them to the poor and come follow him went way sorrowful because he wanted to be an admirer, not a follower. (Matthew 19:16-22) Nowhere do we find Jesus seeking admirers. Jesus gave a commandment to his disciples to "Go therefore and make disciples of all the nations" not admirers of all nations. (Matthew 28:19) Why not an admirer? "The admirer is not willing to make any sacrifices, to give up anything worldly, to reconstruct his life, to be what he admires or let his life express it—but in words, verbal expressions, asseverations, he is inexhaustible in affirming how highly he prizes Christianity."[74] Jesus is calling for disciples who will follow him despite the rejection of the world. Disciples of Christ from the early Christian era to our postmodern times have all experienced rejection. Rejection is one of the devil's greatest and most effective weapon in his arsenal. As difficult as it may be, count it a blessing to be rejected for Jesus Christ. Make rejection your strength and continue to follow Jesus and let the light and life of God shine steadily in you. Shake the dust off your feet and move on with the mission of being followers of Jesus Christ. Shake off the dust of insults, shake off the dust of hatred, shake off the dust of revenge, and other attacks that come your way. Be like the apostles who rejoiced and were counted worthy to suffer shame, dishonor, and rejection for the cause of Jesus Christ. (Acts 5:41)

Deal with rejection the way Jesus did. First, you must put the situation in perspective. You must never personalize and internalize rejection. Rejection says more about those who are doing the rejecting than about you being rejected. Not everyone is going to accept you, and the mission God is accomplishing through you. Keep your focus on what God through Christ is doing through you and leave the rejecters in God's hand. Second, move on when you have been rejected. When Jesus hometown folks rejected him, he continued moved on to accomplish his mission (Mark 6:6)." Jesus remained purpose driven, and you must do likewise. "Oftentimes, rejection by one group results in blessings for others. The rejection of Jesus in his hometown of Nazareth was a blessing for Capernaum. The rejection of Jesus by his own people eventually opened the door for universal redemption. Pauline theology further emphasizes this theme.

---

[74] Ibid., 245.

Because of the rejection of the gospel by the majority of the Jews, salvation was opened to the Gentiles."[75] Regardless the many times you are rejected, know that God is using your rejection as a blessing for others. Mahatma Gandhi gives wise encouragement when you have experienced rejection. "Speak the truth, without fear and without exaggeration, and see everyone whose work is relative to your purpose. You are in God's work, so you need not fear men's scorn. If they listen to your requests, and grant them, you will be satisfied. If they reject them, then you make their rejection your strength."[76]

Never allow rejection to weaken you. Never allow rejection to stop you. Never allow rejection to distract you. In some cases just ignore rejection like Nehemiah did. His opponents rejected the work he was doing, but he would not come down from building the wall to entertain their rejection. Nehemiah responded to his critics by saying, "I am doing a great work and cannot go down. Why should the work cease while I leave it and go down to you (Nehemiah 6:3)." The best way to overcome rejection is to continue the work God is doing in your life. Yes, rejection hurts but deal with it constructively and "Press toward the mark for the prize of the high calling of God in Christ Jesus (Philippians 3:14)." The following hymn can help you follow on with Jesus when you have experienced rejection. It is called Crowning Day by Daniel W. Whittle, 1881.

Our Lord is now rejected,
And by the world disowned,
By the many still neglected,
And by the few enthroned,
But soon He'll come in glory,
The hour is drawing nigh,

---

[75] Mack King Carter, Interpreting the Will of God, Principles for Unlocking the Mystery, Judson Press, 2002, 63.
[76] Cited from Howard Thurman, Deep Is the Hunger, Friends United Press, 1951, 56.

For the crowning day is coming by and by.

Refrain

Oh, the crowning day is coming,
Is coming by and by,
When our Lord shall come "in power,"
And "glory" from on high.
Oh, the glorious sight will gladden,
Each waiting, watchful eye,
In the crowning day that's coming by and by.
The heavens shall glow with splendor,
But brighter far than they
The saints shall shine in glory,
As Christ shall them array,
The beauty of the Savior,
Shall dazzle every eye,
For the crowning day is coming by and by.

Refrain

Our pain shall then be over,
We'll sit and sigh no more,
Behind us all of sorrow,
And naught but joy before,
A joy in our Redeemer,
As we to Him are nigh,
For the crowning day that's coming by and by.

Refrain

Let all that look for, hasten
The coming joyful day,
By earnest consecration,
To walk the narrow way,
By gathering in the lost ones,
For whom our Lord did die,
For the crowning day that's coming by and by.[77]

---

[77] Daniel W. Whittle, "The Crowning Day" 1881, Composer James McGranahan, The Cyber Hymnal, #1102, copyright: Public Domain.

CHAPTER FOUR Expect Criticism

To avoid criticism say nothing, do nothing, be nothing.—Aristotle

Criticism is one of the harsh realities of being a follower of Jesus Christ. Everything you do to bring light to darkness, sweetness to bitterness, love to hate, justice to injustice, and truth to falsehood don't be surprised when criticism knocks on your door. If you are going to be salt and light as Jesus instructed a follower to be, you must prepare for criticism. There is a long line of people who were criticized for doing the will of God. From Moses to the prophets, from Jesus to our present time, criticism was and is a by-product of being a follower of Jesus Christ. You may receive encouragement from your church and community, and God knows followers of Jesus Christ really need encouragement. However, the disclaimer is encouragement is contextual. As long as you do what the context deems is acceptable, you will be encouraged and rewarded. As long as you are in step with the status quo and maintain the culture, pats on the back are acts of approval.

However, once you step outside the culture of your church and your community and follow Jesus in areas that your church and community may not be willing to go, criticism will ensue. Not every church and community is willing to take a risk for Jesus Christ. Not every church and community is serious about modeling their ministry after Jesus who welcomed the poor, the oppressed, the outcast, and the marginalized. Not every church gets involved in making justice a reality for all people. Not every church is serious about eliminating racism, classism, and sexism as a cultural practice. When you decide to follow Jesus and start working against the "isms" that divide people, get ready for criticism. When you decide to become a thermostat rather than a thermometer, prepare for criticism. Following Jesus and taking serious the gospel of the Kingdom of God, you will find out the difference between what many Christians espouse and what they actually practice. Platitudes about love, peace, justice, and equality are wonderful talking points, but try putting them into action and see won't criticism finds its way to your door as it did Jesus.

The reason Jesus was so harshly criticized is he was attacking those things that held people captive. He was preaching and teaching a gospel that was revolutionary certainly not in line with the religious and political structure of his day. Jesus was considered dangerous pointing people to a new way of life and a new consciousness that would break their chains. "The center of Jesus' ministry was the proclamation of a new era: the messianic age. His essential message was. 'Repent, for the Kingdom of heaven is at hand" (Mt. 4:17). He saw himself as the bearer of that Kingdom; he called people to take their stand for him and for the good news that he proclaimed. Jesus' message was first of all religious: it had to do with what God was doing in the world."[78] But, what added fuel to the fire against Jesus was people couldn't pay him off to do what they wanted him to do. You couldn't bribe him; you couldn't flatter him. You couldn't blackmail him. You couldn't trick him, or use any kind of persuasion to get him to deter the course he was on. Jesus was about doing his Father's will, and there was no person off limits to him. It didn't matter if you were a prostitute, a thief, a murderer, a criminal, a hypocrite, a backslider, a whoremonger, a tax collector, or whatever society classified you as Jesus was interested in you. Not only was Jesus interested in you, but he forgave people; he healed people, gave sight to the blind and raised people up from their dead situation. Jesus loved people, and whenever society wrote people off from social acceptance, Jesus wrote

---

[78] Earl H. Brill, The Christian Moral Vision, The Seabury Press, 1979, 49.

them in. When society looked down on people, Jesus looked right at people. When society would push people to the ground, Jesus would lift them up. Jesus came to set people free from the restrictions and limitations that socio-religious structures had imposed upon them. And, just because Jesus loved, healed, fed, forgave, and embraced people of every description, there were critics like the scribes and the Pharisees who hated him for being the kind of leader who really loved and cared about people. When the misfits, the outcasts, the tax collectors, the low lives, the scoundrels, the drunkards, the fornicators, adulterers and great sinners came to hear and eat with Jesus, the scribes and the Pharisees criticized him, saying, "This man receives sinners and he eats with them. (Luke 15:2) They criticized Jesus for healing on the sabbath; they criticized him for plucking corn on the sabbath. They called him "Beelzebul, the prince of devils," and dividing the people. Criticism followed Jesus throughout his ministry.

There are people today like the Pharisees who will criticize you, hate you, talk against you, and sell you out for loving and caring for people. Some people want you to love whom they love and hate who they hate. Some people want you to despise whom they despise and speak against whom they speak against. Because Jesus would not think and act like the Pharisees, they despised and harshly criticized him. However, although Jesus was criticized at every turn, he would not love who you love and hate who you hate. He would not despise whom you despise and talk against whom you talk against. He would not befriend whom you befriend and be an enemy to those you are an enemy with. Jesus had his own mind, and he did his own thinking. Jesus never followed the crowd; he never formed his opinion about people based upon the talk of other people. Jesus was never a thermometer who registered the temperature of society; he never registered prejudice, racism, sexism, ageism, legalism, and other "isms" that people hold against other people. Jesus was a thermostat who set the temperature of society. When Jesus said, "Love your enemies, bless them that curse you, and do good to them that hate you, and pray for them that despitefully use and persecute you," he was setting the temperature of society. When Jesus said, "Whosoever smites you on the right cheek, turn to him the other also," he was setting the temperature of society. Jesus wants you to understand that when you follow him your behavior, attitude, principles, and ethics must be different from the world. In other words, you must have an alternative consciousness than which is of the world.

Not only was Jesus harshly criticized, but anyone who showed appreciation for Jesus was also criticized. One day while Jesus was dining with Simon, the leper, and others, a woman comes up with an alabaster box of precious ointment, and she broke it and poured it on Jesus' head. Matthew, Mark and Luke did not name this woman, but John said it was Mary. (John 12:3) Luke's account of this anointing story is different from Matthew, Mark, and John. Whether we know the name of this woman or not, this woman brings a costly gift of precious ointment and anoints Jesus with it. Her act of kindness generated outrage and criticism among those who were there. Matthew said it was the disciples of Jesus who saw it and had indignation. Jesus own disciples became angry criticizing this woman for her act of kindness. They said it was nothing but a waste (Matthew 26:6-13). It goes without saying that even those in your inner circle will find something in which to criticize you and criticize those who desire to bless you. There are some people who get close to you to help destroy you. They may start out with you but won't end with you because their connection to you had ulterior motives. Jesus said,

"Have I not chosen you, the Twelve? Yet one of you is a devil (John 6:70)!" Not everybody in your inner circle agrees with others blessing you. Many of times they join you to block any blessings that come your way.

69

Thus, very rarely do we find anybody doing anything for Jesus. Out of the many miracles Jesus had done for people, out of all the souls he lifted from the quicksand of hopelessness to the solid rock of possibility, the number of people he fed when they were hungry, the number of blinded eyes he opened, the number of people he healed, the number of dead he raised, the number of people he set free, in return for all of this Jesus received criticism, suspicion, ungratefulness, and resistance. As mighty as he was, as giving as he was, as compassionate as he was, and as loving as he was, the only thing Jesus could say is "Foxes have holes, and birds of the air have nests, but the Son of Man has nowhere to lay his head." (Luke 9:58) Following Jesus is not easy. Out of the many things you do to serve others, do not get offended when all people want is to make withdrawals from you. They are unwilling to make deposits but they are ready to withdraw from you. When Mary came to make a deposit in the life and ministry of Jesus, her act of kindness was criticized. She did not allow the criticism to stop her good deed towards Jesus. She poured the costly ointment on Jesus. Regardless of public criticism, she showed Jesus love and respect. Jesus stopped her critics and said, "Why do you try to make trouble for the woman? She did a fine deed toward me. For you always have the poor with you, but you will not always have me. When she put this perfumed oil on my body, she did it to prepare me for burial. Truly I say to you, wherever this good news is preached in all the world, what this woman has done will also be told in memory of her." (Matthew 26:10-13)

What you do for Jesus Christ, criticism ensues. Pastors are reminded of this all the time. They are constantly criticized for following Jesus Christ. Criticism is synonymous with being a pastor. Kent Crocket explains this in greater detail.

. . . . Satan has always appointed fault-finders to oppose God's leaders. Moses had to deal with his critics in the wilderness who constantly challenged his leadership. Paul was almost killed by his stone-throwing persecutors, and Jesus was crucified by the gnat-straining Pharisees. Common sense would tell you that the miracles they performed authenticated their ministries, but that didn't dissuade their critics.

Ignoring the proof, they kept attacking their innocent targets. . . . Since few people have the guts to stand up to a critic, their nitpicking usually goes unimpeded. Because these abusers show no mercy toward their pastor, God will not let them receive spiritual insight from the one they're judging. As a result, their needs cannot be met-not because the pastor isn't feeding them, but because they have built a wall around their heart which keeps them from receiving from him. This explains why fault-finders will often say, "I'm not getting anything out of the pastor's sermons. . . . I'm not getting my needs met." They'll never be satisfied as long as they continue to criticize their leaders.[79]

Understand that criticism is an effort to get you to give up the journey with Jesus. When others attack you for doing right and standing up for Jesus, don't recant but become more determined to follow Christ. Criticism can cut deeply, but don't allow it to break your spirit. The point here is somewhere on your Christian journey, no matter how hard you work, no matter how hard you sacrifice, and do your best to be a Christian and a faithful follower of Jesus Christ, criticism will find you and do its best to discourage you from following Jesus Christ.

Jesus said, "Woe to you, when all men speak well of you, for their fathers used to do the same things to the false

---

[79] Kent Crockett, Pastor Abusers When Sheep Attack Their Shepherd, Whole Armor Press 2012, 73.

prophets." (Luke 6:26) Regardless of how much we like the praise and approval of others, Jesus is letting you know that if you have not been criticized on your journey, check the road you are traveling because you may be heading the wrong way. The broadway of which many people travel desire for you to live like they live, believe like they believe, and behave like they behave. When people want you to remain with them, they praise you to retain you. As long as you think as they think, and live like they live, no criticism is warranted. This scenario could be in your family, in your church, in your school, in your social group, and in your community. But, as soon as you break loose from the stronghold people have on you, and you start to follow Jesus' will and way, speaking well of you will give way to speaking ill of you. Criticism comes in like a flood. You are criticized because you are going against majority opinion, against consensus, and against a twisted traditional milieu that leaves no room for dissenters. Don't panic when this occurs; it happened to Jesus and the prophets before you. "The messengers of Jesus will be hated to the end of time. They will be blamed for all the divisions which rend cities and homes. Jesus and his disciples will be condemned on all sides for undermining family life, and leading the nation astray; they will be called crazy fanatics, and disturbers of the peace. The disciples will be sorely tempted to desert their Lord."[80]

Therefore, when the storm of criticism blows in your direction, it may bruise you but it can never break you because you now live for Christ who is your shield and defense. When you are being harshly criticized as the friends of Job criticized him for his suffering, hold to your faith in God. Despite the criticism that Job had to endure from his friends, God vindicated Job. "And Jehovah restored the fortunes of Job when he had prayed for his friends. And the

---

[80] Dietrich Bonhoeffer, The Cost of Discipleship, Collier Books Macmillan Publishing Company, 1963, 239.

Lord gave Job twice as much as he had before." 42:10.) Don't allow criticism to destroy you. Take this wise advice from Abraham Lincoln who once said, "If I tried to read, much less answer, all the criticism made of me, and all the attacks leveled against me, this office would have to close for all other business. I do the best I know how, the very best I can. And, I mean to keep on doing this, down to the very end. If the end brings me out all wrong, ten angels swearing I had been right would make no difference. If the end brings me out all right, then what is said against me now will not amount to anything."[81]

This is not to convey that constructive criticism is not good for you because it helps you to assess your shortcomings, strengthens you where you are weak, and show you something about yourself you may not be aware. Constructive criticism is an asset on the Christian journey. A follower of Jesus Christ should never develop an attitude of not welcoming wise and constructive criticism. Jesus had to give his disciples constructive criticism on the journey, and they became better disciples because of it. They became leaders of the Christian movement because Jesus who showed them how to deal with criticism had trained them. If you refuse to humble yourself on this Christian journey, you will not handle criticism well. But, once you humble yourself and yield your heart and mind to Jesus Christ, then you will learn how to handle criticism when it is constructive and destructive. But, be assured you will encounter criticism on your journey. Count on it because it is a fact of following Jesus. When you go outside people's understanding of you and what you stand for, criticism is a by-product. For example, "The giants of history have been men and women who dared say what they thought, despite the snarl of the mob. Emerson the people called crazy, Napoleon they

---

[81] Cited in The Speaker's Book of Illustrations by Herbert V. Prochnow, Baker Book House, 1960, 40.

ridiculed, Luther they fought, Columbus they branded a witless adventurer, Wagner they hounded from place to place, Lincoln they black-guarded, Jesus they crucified. Yet these lonely figures, robbed of appreciation, were to be envied —not pitied."[82] How you handle criticism will speak volumes. Below is a hymn by William H. Clark and refrain by Ralph E. Hudson, to help you through your time of criticism.

All praise to God who reigns above
In majesty supreme,
Who gave His Son for all to die,
That He might all redeem!

Refrain:

Blessed be the name! Blessed be the name!
Blessed be the name of the Lord!
Blessed be the name! Blessed be the name!
Blessed be the name of the Lord!
His name above all names shall stand,
Exalted more and more,
He's seated at God's own right hand,
Where angel hosts adore.

Refrain:

Blessed be the name! Blessed be the name!
Blessed be the name of the Lord!
Blessed be the name! Blessed be the name!
Blessed be the name of the Lord!
Redeemer, Savior, friend of all
Once ruined by the fall,
Thou hast devised salvation's call,
For Thou hast died for all.

Refrain:

Blessed be the name! Blessed be the name!

---

[82] Edward Earle Puritan, The Triumph of the Man Who Acts, Efficiency Publishing Company, 1916, 121.

Blessed be the name of the Lord!
Blessed be the name! Blessed be the name!
Blessed be the name of the Lord!
His name shall be the Counselor,
The mighty Prince of Peace,
Of all earth's kingdoms conqueror,
Whose reign shall never cease.

Refrain:

Blessed be the name! Blessed be the name!
Blessed be the name of the Lord!
Blessed be the name! Blessed be the name!
Blessed be the name of the Lord![83]

---

[83] William H. Clark, Reframe by Ralph E. Hudson, "Blessed Be the Name," arr. by Nolan Williams, Jr., 2000, GIA Publications, Inc.

CHAPTER FIVE Expect Loneliness

Snuggle in God's arms. When you are hurting, when you feel lonely, left out. Let Him cradle you, comfort you, reassure you of His all-sufficient power and love.—Kay Arthur

One of the most challenging realities of following Jesus Christ is to embrace loneliness. At times, you will experience loneliness on this journey because your walk with Christ makes you radically different from people of the world. You may feel a sense of loneliness among other people because your relationship with Jesus Christ is serious. You may even experience profound loneliness among Christians who are Christians by name only. Cultural Christians may think and feel it is all right to mingle and mimic the lifestyles, acts, and behaviors of this sinful world. Because of the convictions, you hold as a follower of Jesus Christ, these convictions will not allow you to be indistinguishable from the world. You cannot sit at the Lord's table and the devil's table as some Christians are doing. You are radically different. You are distinguishable from others. A follower of Jesus Christ should always be distinguishable from the world, and since you take your walk with Christ serious, this brings on loneliness.

A.W. Tozer said, "The weakness of so many modern Christians is that they feel too much at home in the world. In their effort to achieve restful 'adjustment' to unregenerate society they have lost their pilgrim character and become an essential part of the very moral order against which they are sent to protest. The world recognizes them and accepts them for what they are. And this is the saddest thing than can be said about them. They are not lonely, but neither are they saints."[84] So, understand then that loneliness is the price you pay for following Jesus Christ. But, be of good cheer

---

[84] A. W. Tozer, Man The Dwelling Place of God, Fig Publisher, 2012, 144.

loneliness does not mean you are alone. Jesus promised, "I am with you always, even to the end of the age." (Matthew 28:20) Do not let loneliness get you down; take advantage of loneliness; it is an opportunity to pray, to read God's Word, and allow Christ's presence to ministry to you. So make loneliness your friend not your enemy. It is how you respond to loneliness that makes the difference.

It is understood that loneliness can affect people in many different ways. Some people have been physically, emotionally and spiritually damaged by loneliness. Some people have died due to loneliness. Some have developed psychological problems. Rejection, divorce, unwanted, unneeded, unnecessary, and the loss of a loved one can induce painful feelings of loneliness. People who have been married for several years and one of the spouses dies; loneliness is a tough situation to overcome. When people no longer feel socially connected, loneliness can be unbearable. Without question as human beings, we were not made to be alone in this world. We hunger for affection; we hunger for company; we hunger for social connection because John Donne stated, "No person is an island." We were made to be connected, and when this connection has been severed, loneliness can lead to sadness, depression, and death. Having said this, followers of Jesus Christ are not in denial about loneliness. They embrace loneliness and respond to it creatively and constructively because for a follower of Jesus Christ loneliness does not mean being alone. The reason followers of Jesus Christ don't crack up due to loneliness is their connection to God. Their vertical connection to God helps with the horizontal connection with those on the same journey, and with the disconnection with those who are not. Vertical connection to God is key in dealing with horizontal connection and disconnection.

For example, John the Baptist lived in the wilderness of solitude during his ministry. Because of his vertical connection to God, this caused a horizontal disconnection with the world of sin and evil. John experienced loneliness, but he knew he was not alone. He preached and baptized alone encouraging people to repent because the axe was laid at the root of the tree. Due to his radical preaching, this brought about loneliness because no one else was preaching like John. His indictment of Herod and the Roman Empire did not attract friends to him. Although he had a few disciples, John spent most of his public life in loneliness. Because he was not popular with the religious and political structure of his day nor would he go alone to get alone, this rendered him loneliness of which he handled very well. You will not handle loneliness well if you don't have a connection with God. Many people go alone to avoid loneliness. They would rather be in the crowd than to be alone with their conscience. John the Baptist is one life that should teach you that it is better to be alone with a good consciousness than to be in the company of others with a bad conscious. Many people cannot handle loneliness. They enter into depression, sadness, and death because they are not really vertically connected to God.

It is often said, "The higher you climb in life, the lonelier you become." All his life Jesus climbed the mountain of total obedience to God. He climbed the heights of love, truth, and forgiveness that put him at odds with the whole world. Because of his higher wisdom, higher ethics, higher allegiance, and higher patriotism, this brought on loneliness even while being with his disciples who at times could not understand him. Throughout his ministry, Jesus took time to be alone in solitude with God. Solitude with God keeps you grounded; it keeps you focus on your mission, and gives you strength for the journey. Too often followers of Christ get distracted because they are so overworked, so busy, and don't have enough time to pray, read the Scriptures, and reconnect with themselves and with their Lord. Their busyness has become an enemy to their relationship with Jesus Christ. If they are not careful, busyness can be a weapon the devil can use to help them lose their solitude that is necessary to stay connected to God. This is why being alone in solitude with God can help followers of Jesus Christ stay on the straight and narrow path. Loneliness with God can help you bear your cross when others around you don't understand the path you have decided to take.

Some of the best insights, wisdom, and encounters with God have come through being alone in solitude. For example, "Religious ideas have come to us from the wilderness, from mountain tops, from dens and caves, and from the vast spaces from which come the mirage and other shadowy illusions which create rivers, lakes, and forests where there are none. The song of angels could be better heard by the shepherds on the plains of Bethlehem than by the jostling crowds in the busy streets of Jerusalem. John the Baptist could preach better in the wilderness than in the busy marts of men. Jesus said his best word to the world when on the Mount of Olives. Moses learned more of the laws of God when in the mountains than when down among the people. The Hebrew prophets frequented dens and caves and desert places. John saw his wonderful vision in the Isle of Patmos with naught in sight but the sea and sky. It was in a lonely place that Jacob wrestled with the angel. The Transfiguration was on a mountain. No wonder that Moses wandering in the vast and silent desert, after killing an Egyptian and brooding over the oppressed condition of his people, should hear the voice of Jehovah saying, "I have seen the affliction of my people." Paul was not in Damascus, but on his lonely way thither, when he heard a voice from heaven. The heart beats louder, and the soul hears quicker in silence and solitude."[85] So, take advantage of the loneliness when it is the result of following Jesus in a world of scorn.

---

[85] Frederick Douglass, Life and Times, New York: Collier Books, MacMillan Publishing Company, 1962, 583.

When Martin Luther King, Jr. made the decision to speak out against the Vietnam War, he experienced a profound loneliness because many around him advised him not to do it. But, he was willing to bear this cross because of his solitude with God who gave him the strength to do what others were unwilling to do. A follower of Jesus Christ must "Always remember: you cannot carry a cross in company. Though a man was surrounded by a vast crowd, his cross is his alone and his carrying of it marks him as a man apart. Society has turned against him; otherwise, he would have no cross. No one is a friend to the man with a cross."[86] When loneliness is the result of you doing what God is calling you to do, bear your cross; bear it for truth; bear it for justice; bear it for righteousness. You are bearing a cross because you have decided to travel the narrow way that leads to eternal life. Only a few travel the narrow way and now and then they find a fellow traveler. Remember what Jesus said, "Enter through the narrow gate; for the gate is wide and the way is broad that leads to destruction, and there are many who enter through it. For the gate is small and the way is narrow that leads to life, and there are few who find it." (Matthew 7:13-14) While traveling on the narrow way do not be surprised nor in despair about long periods of loneliness before you find another traveler on the way. Loneliness does not equate to being alone; it means you have decided not to follow the crowds of the world while following Jesus Christ. This decision is tough and costs you something; but in the final analysis, it is worth it.

Please understand that Jesus not only knows about loneliness; he experienced it. Out of all the preaching, teaching, and miracles he performed, you would think that Jesus wouldn't have feeling of being alone; but, he did. He said, "Foxes have holes, and birds of the air have nests, but the Son of Man has nowhere to lay his head." (Luke 9:58)

---

[86] A. W. Tozer, Man The Dwelling Place of God 142.

Jesus felt profound loneliness. When he was in the garden of Gethsemane praying to God to see if there was another way for the redemption of mankind, he felt a profound loneliness that no one else could understand. He prayed to God to let the cup pass from him. "Father, if you are willing, remove this cup from me. Nevertheless, not my will, but yours, be done." (Luke 22:42) Jesus knew that sin is separation from God, and he was about to take on the sins of the whole world. To bear the cross for the sins of the whole world was a loneliness that no one else could bear or understand. But, Jesus went through with it because not only did he have profound love for humanity, he had total faith and truth in God to give him the victory over it. The way of redemption was lonely, but he traveled it. When they lead him from judgment hall to judgment hall, he was alone. When they publicly beat him and placed a crown of thorns on his head, he was alone. When the people shouted crucify him, crucify him, he was alone. When they placed a cross on his shoulders and had him to carry it through the streets of Jerusalem, he was alone. When they nailed him to the cross, and he cried, "My God, My God, why have You forsaken Me?" (Matthew 27:46) He was alone. During the most darkest hour in his life, Jesus felt alone, forsaken by God, disciples, those he healed, fed, and raised from the dead. He was the world's loneliest Savior. Yet, he has the audacity to say, "Follow Me."

Since a servant is no greater than his master, you too will find yourself in your respective Gethsemane, in which you are faced with a bitter cup. Every follower of Jesus has a bitter cup to drink. The bitter cup of loneliness, rejection, criticism, misunderstanding, abandonment and death is what a follower must drink to follow Jesus Christ. Your bitter cup is usually lonely. Your Gethsemane is lonely because it is a place that no one can understand what you are going through and what you are facing except another follower who is experiencing the same thing. Although family and friends may be around you, but if they are not true followers of

Jesus Christ, they cannot understand what you are really going through. Gethsemane is where you are wrestling with yourself, your loneliness, and submitting your life to the will of God. You must remember that you are a stranger and pilgrim traveling through this life of darkness, sin, and death. Because you are in the world and not of the world, you must embrace the loneliness that comes with being a pilgrim traveler. This world is not your home. You are passing through it onto God's Kingdom of which Jesus is preparing for you to live with him forever.

Jesus wants you to be resolved in following him. Don't let the loneliness deter you from the course of following Jesus. He wants you to understand that life consists of two paths and you must choose which one you will travel. The first path is described as the wide gate. The nonspiritual gate. Many people go through the wide gate and travel on the broad road. They live like they want because they view freedom as living without constraints, without responsibility, and insisting on their rights of autonomy. The wide gate and the broad road accommodate people who want rights without righteousness. They accommodate sexual immorality, robbery, trickery, thievery, murder, lying, stealing, evil, injustice, and haters of God. The wider the gate the more inviting it is. The wide gate welcomes unethical politicians; it welcomes uncaring CEOs. It throws parties for Wall Street and invites Main Street. It has room for greedy and deceiving preachers. It greets power hungry deacons; it welcomes shady living choir members; it beckons for lukewarm Christians and those who want to be accepted by the world. Jesus reminds us that this wide gate has many travelers: politicians, CEO's, preachers pastors, deacons, lay people, and people of every description. The path is broad and leads to destruction.

Then Jesus describes another path, which he calls the strait gate. The strait gate is least traveled, and those who are on this path can get mighty lonely sometimes. It gets mighty discouraging sometimes because people criticize you; people talk against you; people misunderstand you; people don't support you, and call you everything but a child of God. The strait and narrow way mean bearing a cross along the way. The narrow way is about discipline and commitment. It is about being true and honest, just and pure, loving and of good report. It requires obedience and self-denial. It requires seeking first the Kingdom of God. The narrow path is not easy to travel. There are hills and mountains; there are steep curves, rough overpasses, and dangerous embankments. But Jesus wants you to understand that although you will experience loneliness on the straight and narrow path, it does lead to eternal life and wholeness.

In conclusion, God used many people differently in the Bible. One thing that was common to them all was loneliness. They all at times felt profound loneliness, but they never lost their solitude with God. You must never lose solitude with God because this is what will get you through your times of loneliness. To put it all in perspective A.W. Tozer gives an indelible insight on the subject of loneliness. He said, "The pain of loneliness arises from the constitution of our nature. God made us for each other. The desire for human companionship is completely natural and right. The loneliness of the Christian results from his walk with God in an ungodly world, a walk that must often take him away from the fellowship of good Christians as well as from that of the unregenerate world. His God-given instincts cry out for companionship with others of his kind, others who can understand his longings, his aspirations, his absorptions in the love of Christ; and because within his circle of friends therefore so few who share his inner experiences he is forced to walk alone."[87]

The following hymn should help you keep on keeping on during times of loneliness:

I come to the garden alone, While the

---

[87] Ibid., 142-143.

dew is still on the roses; And the voice I hear,
falling on my ear, The Son of God discloses
And He walks with me, and He talks with me,
And He tells me I am His own, And the joy we share
as we tarry there, None other has ever known.
He speaks, and the sound of His voice Is so
sweet the birds hush their singing; And the melody
that He gave to me With-in my heart is ringing.
And He walks with me, and He talks with me,
And He tells me I am His own, And the joy we share
as we tarry there, None other has ever known.
I'd stay in the garden with Him Though the
night around me be falling; But He bids me go
through the voice of woe, His voice to me is calling.
And He walks with me, and He talks with me,
And He tells me I am His own, And the joy we share
as we tarry there, None other has ever known.[88]

---

[88] Cited from African American Heritage Hymnal, GIA Publication, INC. Chicago, 2001, Text: C. Austin Miles, 1868-1946, Tune: Garden, 89107 with refrain, 494.

CHAPTER SIX Expect Betrayal

Psalm 41:9 Updated American Standard Version (UASV)

⁹ Even my close friend in whom I trusted,
  who ate my bread, has lifted his heel against me.

There is nothing like the betrayal of family, friends, and countrymen. Betrayal cuts deeply, and it makes it difficult for people to put trust in others again. Betrayal can damage human relations for many years to come. It is a defect in the human character of many people. You don't expect those you love, grew up with, went to school with, struggled with, and do ministry with ever to betray you. But, history reveals that betrayal has been part of the human drama since ancient times, and it will continue to be part of human history. People betray each other for various reasons; nevertheless, it is still betrayal. Just as Jesus was betrayed, you must expect betrayal as a follower of Jesus Christ. You must expect that there is a Judas somewhere among people who will betray you. Your Judas may not yet be revealed, but as time goes on and events occur, your betrayer will become visible. The people who will betray you may not intend to betray you or ever believe that they could do such a thing because the time has not come for things to be shaken up around you. When that time comes, your betrayers will be exposed. How you handle your betrayal will reveal how serious you take your discipleship as a follower of Jesus Christ. It is not easy living with betrayal. It is a hard pill to swallow and a deep wound to heal but on this journey expect betrayal.

There is no doubt that "Betrayal is a destructive force that leaves many ruins in its path. Betrayal changes everything. Relationships and all those affected will never be the same. The damage done can be irreparable. Trust is lost. Wounds run deep. Anger persists. Hearts are broken. Self-protective walls are erected. Pain is long and lasting. And we wonder . . . Can trust ever be restored? Do wounds ever heal? Will anger cease to exist? Can hearts be repaired? Will the self-protective walls ever come down? Does the pain ever go away?"[89] The answer to these questions is a resounding Yes! Betrayal does not have to hold you captive for the rest of your life. You can heal from it; you can grow from it, and you can overcome its devastating effects.

Those whom God used in His salvation plan have experienced betrayal. Betrayal is ugly in all its dimensions. However, if you trust in God and not allow bitterness to eat away at your soul, you can overcome the traumatic effects of betrayal. Getting over betrayal won't be easy but with God's help, you cannot only survive but also thrive. It is important to make sure that you remain obedient to God because once you go outside the will of God, betrayal may be impossible to overcome. For example, when Samson was told not to reveal the secret of where his strength lies, he obeyed until he met Delilah. When Delilah put her charm on Samson, and he finally told the secret of where his strength lies, she betrayed him. You cannot operate outside the will of God and think your life will remain the same. After revealing the secret of where his strength lies, Samson said, "I will go out as at other times and shake myself free." But he did not know that Jehovah had left him." (Judges 16:20) Betrayal caused his eyes to be gouged out, and he was thrown in prison. Although the Lord forgave Samson and restored his strength, Samson died with his enemies. The secret of Samson's strength was not really in Samson's hair. His strength was in the Lord. When you forget where your strength lies, it is very difficult to overcome betrayal.

Another example of betrayal is a man named Joseph who was betrayed by his own brothers. Just because Joseph was a gifted dreamer, a favorite of his father, and was given a coat of many colors, his brothers became jealous and angry

---

[89] Krystal Kuehn, "Betrayal: When Someone You Love Betrays You," Published on SelfGrowth.com, September 23, 2010.

with Joseph. It never dawned on Joseph that his brothers would ever betray him. The brothers probably never thought that they would do such a thing. But, when Joseph spoke about his dreams and how his brothers would bow to him, he didn't know this was causing resentment in his brothers. Joseph was only communicating his dreams; he didn't know the implications of his dreams nor did he know what he would have to go through for these dreams to become a reality. The jealousy that builds up over time caused Joseph's brothers to betray him, and they sold him to be a slave in Egypt. Not only did the brothers betray Joseph but they betrayed their Father Jacob by conveying to him that Joseph was torn to pieces by a wild animal. Jacob went through anguish because his sons betrayed him. While in Egypt, Joseph went through hell. Not only did his brothers betray him, but also Potiphar's wife betrayed him by lying on him. Joseph was thrown in prison and spent many years there before he was elevated to prime minister. He had a long time to think about the betrayals in his life, and it is certain that he deeply resented his betrayers for what they had done. But, Joseph never operated outside the will of God; he allowed God to deal with him and his betrayers as you must do when following Jesus Christ.

Keep in mind that whenever God has gifted you to impact the world, others will try to control you, and when they cannot control you, they will seek to destroy you. The devil doesn't mind your gift because there is nothing he can do about it because it is God given. But, what the devil can do is try to keep you from using your gift to do the will of God. Sometimes, those you have put your trust in may be the very ones the devil may use to keep you from using your gift to impact the world for Christ. The betrayal of friends and loved ones can stifle you from using your gift. This is why you must not wallow in the pain and agony of betrayal. You must accept the betrayal as a reality, respond to it creatively and lovingly, but never allow it to stop you from doing the will of God. Yes, it hurts; yes, it is painful; yes it can knock you down in disbelief that you have been betrayed, but get up and move on to complete your spiritual assignment. Again, betrayal is to be expected following Jesus. You never know who is around you as a wolf in sheep clothing. This is not to make you paranoid but to prepare you when betrayal knocks on your door. When it does, you must not allow this to deter you from following Jesus nor fulfilling the destiny of your life.

There was no doubt that Joseph was upset with his brothers, but he didn't allow this to handicap his life. Joseph produced despite his betrayals. He allowed himself to love and be loved. He got married and had two children. Betrayal bruised him, but it didn't break him. Dr. Laura Schlessinger said, "The greatest source of misunderstanding for a large percentage of betrayed people is that when they stay immersed in their unhappiness about being betrayed, they, in turn, betray all the wonderful people who love and stand by them. Husbands and wives who spend their time depressed and anxious about their problems with a betrayer rob their families of the love and attention they would be giving them if they were not so focused on the betrayer."[90] Over a process of time, God not only brought salvation to Egypt but to Joseph's whole family as well. Looking back on his betrayals, Joseph saw the hand of God working out the salvation of his people. Joseph identified the silver lining in his betrayals, and said to his brothers who betrayed him, "You intended to harm me, but God intended it for good to accomplish what is now being done, the saving of many lives." Blessings often time come in disguises. It is good to reflect on what got you through the hard times. God allowed things to happen to you in order to position you to do His

---

[90] Dr. Laura Schlessinger, Surviving A Shark Attack On Land: Overcoming Betrayal and Dealing with Revenge, An Imprint of HarperCollins Publishers, 2011, 154.

will even with those who have betrayed you. Dr. Laura Schlessinger said, "If you are so bogged down with hurt and rage over a betrayal, then you might miss out on what could possibly change your life forever—and in the most positive way."[91] Joseph let go his hurt and rage of betrayal, and this changed his life forever. Betrayal of people is not the end of the world; it could be a new beginning in which you discover things about yourself you never knew before. Gifts that are lying dormant in you have to be drawn out, and sometimes through hurtful situations and circumstances a new you emerge. This is not to excuse the betrayer nor negate the pain and agony that comes with being betrayed. It is to help you put things in perspective and allow God to lead you through the betrayal and heal you of it.

Therefore, the betrayal of people should not lead followers of Jesus Christ to getting revenge. God will use the betrayal of people for your benefit; and God knows better how to work through situations and circumstances far better than you do. Just as God used the betrayal of Joseph's brothers and the betrayal of Judas and others into God's overall purpose, God will use your betrayal to work in His overall plan as well. So, when you are betrayed, don't get bent out of shape and lose your self-control because you are in God's plan. God's plans have twists and turns, ups and downs, and when people think they are hurting you by their betrayal, somehow they are helping you to reach the heights God has for you. Remember, no one can outmaneuver God. God knows how to bring good out of evil. Learning to trust God is key when you have been betrayed.

This does not mean that God has planned for people to betray you. This means that when people do betray you, God will turn it for your good. Understand, God knows that betrayal hurts; it cuts deeply, and when it comes from family and dear friends, it can be unbearable. But, through the grace

---

[91] Ibid., 174.

of God, you will overcome it and achieve what God has chosen you to do. Don't allow the betrayal of others to stifle your purpose and mission in life. As hurtful as it is don't allow betrayal to cause you to become bitter and you lose your focus on what God is calling you to do. When bitterness enters your spirit, it affects your health and your psychological wellbeing. It is understood that when you find out that you have been betrayed, your initial feelings are shock, anger, and revenge. But, you must take control of these feelings because once you become bitter and get set on revenge, those who betrayed you are now controlling you. The best way to overcome betrayal is not to allow it to control your life. Joseph did not allow the betrayal of his brothers to cause him to miss the opportunity to not only be great but to do great things for the Kingdom of God. Betrayal did not win. Love and forgiveness won. "When goodness follows the betrayal, people are drawl to you, and your opportunities for healthy support and surprising events are more likely."[92]

Jesus knew we would be betrayed just as he was betrayed. Judas betrayed Jesus for thirty pieces of silver. After receiving the traitor's kiss, Jesus responded by calling Judas a friend (Matthew 26:50). Jesus didn't curse him or strike him in any way. Jesus allowed love to convict Judas. Allowing love to operate instead of the pain we feel when we are betrayed speaks volumes of our maturity as a disciple of Jesus Christ. Jesus was trying to reach Judas even though Jesus knew that Judas would betray him. Jesus had the heart to forgive even a traitor, which is an example for us to follow. As hard as this may be, followers of Jesus must forgive traitors. Followers cannot do this in their own ability; it must be done with the power of God. The window of forgiveness and reconciliation was open to the last minutes of Judas life. Judas chose to hang himself because the love that Jesus

---

[92] Ibid,. 184.

demonstrated toward him by calling him friend shook his conscience to the point that guilt took over and caused him to destroy himself. It is often said, "the conscience cannot endure much violence." All Judas had to do was to repent, and Jesus would have forgiven him and accepted him back into the fold of disciples as Jesus did with Peter who denied him.

However, before you condemn Judas for his betrayal, look at yourself. Do an introspection of yourself. We all have been betrayers in one way or another. People never think that silence concerning wrong, evil, and injustice is also a form of betrayal. When you are silent in the midst of people being mistreated, abused, and beaten down by the forces of injustice, you are a betrayer. Those who don't have a voice and you have the power and opportunity to speak for them, and you refuse to do so, you are a betrayer. When you refuse to speak a kind and loving word to those who desperately need to know that they matter, you are a betrayer. Silence in the midst of institutional and structural racism, you are a betrayer. Silence concerning spousal and child abuse, you are a betrayer. Silence in the midst of innocent people going to prison, and you have the evidence to prevent wrongful convictions; you are a betrayer. Many murders are roaming free in communities across the nation because people are afraid to speak up. Their silence is a betrayal to not only the Kingdom of God but to democracy as well. It is a sad commentary that the postmodern church is silent on issues that really matters to the Kingdom of God. Justice and righteousness matter to the Kingdom of God. Getting rid of the causes of poverty, hunger, nakedness, and homelessness matters to the Kingdom of God. But, when you and I are silent about these things, we are betrayers of Jesus Christ and the Kingdom of God. History should teach us that when we are silent about issues that really matters, tyranny gets worse. Had the church of Germany spoken out against the evils and injustice of Hitler's regime, may be six million people could have been spared from the gas chambers that took their lives. "If we keep Christ to ourselves out of fear of reprisals, are we not taking our stand with those pastors in Germany who chose to close ranks with Hitler? Is not our sin even greater since the consequences of our obedience to Christ are so minimal in comparison with what they faced? Are we qualified to sit in judgment of the Church in Germany if we ourselves have never lost a job or failed a course because we are Christians?"[93]

There are many issues in life in which Christians remain silent that our nation and the nations of the world will pay a heavy price for it. So, while you try to heal from betrayal, don't forget as you are struggling with forgiveness, God through Jesus Christ has forgiven you for your betrayal in the past, and the betrayal you may be demonstrating today by your silence on issues that really matters to the Kingdom of God. As you deal with the betrayal on this Christian journey, the following hymn called "Jesus, Keep Me Near The Cross" can help you overcome it.

> Jesus, keep me near the cross;
>   there a precious fountain,
>   free to all, a healing stream,
>   flows from Calvary's mountain.

Refrain:
In the cross, in the cross,
be my glory ever,
till my raptured soul shall find
rest beyond the river.
  Near the cross, a trembling soul,
love and mercy found me;
there the bright and morning star
sheds its beams around me.

---

93 Erwin W. Lutzer, When A Nation Forget God, Moody Publishers, 2010, 120.

(Refrain)

Near the cross! O Lamb of God,
bring its scenes before me;
help me walk from day to day
with its shadow o'er me.

(Refrain)

Near the cross I'll watch and wait,
hoping, trusting ever,
till I reach the golden strand
just beyond the river.[94]

(Refrain)

---

[94] Fanny J. Crosby, 1869 "Near the Cross," Music by William H. Doane, 1869, The United Methodist Hymnal, The United Methodist Publishing House, 1989, 301.

CHAPTER SEVEN Expect Persecution

Never did the church so much prosper and so truly thrive as when she was baptized in the blood. The ship of the church never sails so gloriously along as when bloody spray of her martyrs falls on her deck. We must suffer and we must die, if we are ever to conquer this world for Christ.—Charles Spurgeon.

It is a known fact that the Christian faith we participate in started in conflict and it shall end in conflict. The Christian faith is in conflict with the world. The values, principles, and ethics followers of Jesus Christ believe and practice are not embraced by the world. The world loves its own. Jesus said, "If you were of the world, the world would love you as its own; but because you are not of the world, but I chose you out of the world, therefore the world hates you. Remember the word that I said to you: 'A slave[95] is not greater than his master.' If they persecuted me, they will also persecute you. If they kept my word, they will keep yours also." (John 15:19-20) Followers of Christ are in a difficult situation. Due to the fact that two Kingdoms are operating at the same time in the world, followers of Christ are on a tightrope. They are citizens of the Kingdom of this world and of the Kingdom of God. Trying to balance the two and remain responsible in both kingdoms that are diametrically opposing to each other is a daunting task, to say the least. Just as Jesus was trying to keep a balance between the old Jewish law and the emerging new covenant of love and grace but was persecuted for trying to usher in the latter, so will the followers of Christ be persecuted.

---

[95] Or *servant*

When followers of Christ decide to hold to the higher patriotism of the Kingdom of God and practice civil disobedience when necessary, break injunctions that are out of harmony with the Kingdom of God, persecution comes as a result of this conflict. The early Christians suffered persecution because they were willing to "Obey God rather than men." (Acts 5:29) They willingly suffered persecution that others might turn to God. Suffering persecution for Christ is redemptive. "What is redemptive suffering? It is voluntary suffering that wipes out the individual but saves the community. It is meritorious, not because of the injury done to the individual, but because of the blessings that are bequeathed to the group. This is not fatalism. It is, rather, the genius of God in transforming suffering into salvation."[96] Therefore, to follow Jesus Christ is to hold allegiance to the Kingdom of God higher than any earthly kingdom, and in doing so no follower will get through this life unscathed.

The Scripture teaches, "All who desire to live godly in Christ Jesus will be persecuted." (2 Timothy 3:12) The resistance of the world to the gospel of Jesus Christ will continue, and so will the persecution. Because the world does not know God nor his Son, followers of Jesus Christ must understand that they are strangers and pilgrims on planet earth who are different. We have different ethics, values, and a different worldview that puts us at odds with the world. But, God through Christ wants to use our being different in the world to make a difference. Knowing very well that living godly will bring persecution, it is what God chooses to make Himself known to others. Don't be ashamed that you are called in Christ to be different in the world. Colleen Townsend Evans makes this poignant observation. "Most people are suspicious of those who are different. The person who radically follows Jesus is different. It is not easy to have

---

[96] Mack King Carter, Interpreting the Will of God Principles for Unlocking the Mystery, Judson Press, 2002, 46.

the courage to stand up and be counted as Christians when we know ahead of time we will be judged unkindly. The world is not comfortable with goodness; it can even be dangerous to be good. Nonconformity is suspect. The world—that is, a society without God—would be more comfortable with everybody fitting into its mold. But as followers of Christ, we are told not to fit into the world's mold but to submit ourselves to be made like Him. Being different is difficult—risky—and yet the Kingdom demands that we take that risk. If we are not different people, we are probably not abiding in union with Jesus."[97]

As disconcerting as it is, and contrary to what many Christians have been taught, following Jesus Christ is tantamount to suffering. If Christians are not suffering persecution on some level, then Christians need to reassess to see if they are really following Jesus Christ. Could it be that many have become cultural Christians rather than followers of Jesus Christ? Could it be that many Christians have cheapened the grace of God? Could it be that so many Christians are fixated on prosperity that they have lost the purpose and power to suffer for the gospel? Have the cares of this world desensitized Christians to the point that they are siding with the powerful against the powerless? Is it possible that Christians are more in love in security than salvation? Whatever the answer is to these questions, the core problem is many Christians avoid persecution because they are more in love with themselves than with Jesus Christ. They have not denied themselves nor picked up their cross to follow Jesus. Avoiding persecution is not only avoiding the call but also avoiding conforming to the likeness of Jesus Christ. It just may be that God allows great persecution to come to the church to purge it of phonies, purify it of selfishness, and expose its hypocrisy. Persecution can serve as a cleaning agent

---

[97] Colleen Townsend Evans, The Vine Life, Chosen Books Publishing Company, 1980, 114.

to not only clean up the saints and direct them back to their purpose but to also win sinners to Jesus Christ.

Postmodern followers of Christ can learn from the early Christians; they dared to follow and believe in the Son of God. It was by his name that miracles were performed and salvation was offered to them that believed. The early Christians were willing to suffer persecution than to deny Jesus Christ. They said to the Jewish religious leaders, who were commanding them to stop preaching about Jesus, "But Peter and John answered them, "Whether it is right in the sight of God to listen to you rather than to God, you must judge; for we cannot stop speaking about what we have seen and heard." (Acts 4:19-20) When the apostles were beaten in public for speaking and performing miracles in Jesus name, and told by the religious authorities not to speak anymore in Jesus name, they departed rejoicing that they were worthy to suffer persecution in Jesus name. (Acts 6:40-41) The early Christians were willing to suffer persecution to bear witness that Jesus Christ is Lord. Many were tortured. "Others received their trial by mockings and scourgings, indeed, more than that, by chains and prisons. They were stoned, they were tried, they were sawn in two, they were slaughtered by the sword, they went about in sheepskins, in goatskins, destitute, afflicted, and mistreated; and the world was not worthy of them. They wandered about in deserts and mountains and caves and dens of the earth." (Hebrews 11:36-38) They knew that persecution would come as a result of embracing the gospel of Jesus Christ, but what was fascinating they rejoiced willing to pay the price for this radical gospel that was turning the world right side up inside out. "Willingly they sacrificed fame, fortune, and life itself in behalf of a cause they knew to be right. Quantitatively small, they were qualitatively giants. Their powerful gospel put an end to such barbaric evils as infanticide and bloody gladiatorial contests. Finally, they captured the Roman Empire for Jesus Christ."[98]

Today in these postmodern times, if followers want to transform the culture for Christ, they must understand that persecution is woven within the process of being a witness for Jesus Christ. Taking a stand for Christ in a culture gone wild in ungodliness won't be easy. Pressure from society will bear down on you. When you make a decision to take a stand for Christ against the culture, get ready because persecution is coming. Don't be surprised where this persecution may come from. It may come from your family, friends, church, denomination, school, community, and those who claimed to know God. Persecution can come in many ways. It can come through censorship, verbal and physical attacks, propaganda, bullying, denial of rights and services, ostracized, etc. Depending on where you are living and how hostile the environment is against Jesus Christ will determine the form of persecution you will suffer. When you are persecuted, remember what Peter said to the early Christians who were undergoing persecution:

Dear friends, do not be surprised at the fiery ordeal that has come on you to test you, as though something strange were happening to you. But, rejoice inasmuch as you participate in the suffering of Christ, so that you may be overjoyed when his glory is revealed. If you are insulted because of the name of Christ, you are blessed, for the Spirit of glory and of God rests on you. If you suffer, it should not be as a murder or thief or any other kind of criminal, or even as a meddler. However, if you suffer as a Christian, do not be ashamed, but praise God that you bear that name. (1 Peter 4:12-16)

Therefore, let there be no doubt that when you publicly bring to bear Christ on the culture, you will bring down

---

[98] Martin Luther King , Jr., Strength to Love, Fortress Press, 1963, 22.

persecution upon you for doing so. The Scriptures are replete with examples of people who decided to take the risk for God and leave the consequences in God's hand. Daniel and his three companions decided to take the risk. The prophets and the early Christians decided to take the risk and leave the consequences in God's hand. In the United States people like Abraham Lincoln, William Lloyd Garrison, Frederick Douglass, Harriet Tubman, Rosa Parks, Martin Luther King, Jr., etc. decided to take a risk for justice and righteousness and left the consequences in God's hand. There is no gainsaying that our nation is the better for what these Christians and others decided to do in an empire that needed salvation and transformation. Once again, America must be challenged because our land is seriously sick, and followers of Christ must be willing to suffer persecution to bring Christ to bear on the culture if redemption is to come to the American empire. What happens in America affects the whole world. Jesse Yow puts it bluntly:

> Hostility and persecution against Christians seem to be growing in the United States and, with a few exceptions, in other countries worldwide. U.S. has been trending in this direction for years as the nation becomes more secular and as Christianity's influence on culture and society wanes. Thus, Christians in North America face increasing pressure to keep their faith to themselves—to practice Christianity in private and not speak of Jesus in public. Such pressure affects churches as well as individuals. It comes through covert or overt censorship, claims that speaking God's Word constitutes hate speech, accusations of hypocrisy and bigotry, and similar forms of hostility. These trends seem to have gone further and perhaps in a slightly different direction in Europe, where Christians face opposition from religious institutions and secular organizations alike, and state churches often stand nearly empty as relics from when

Christianity thrived. Even worse, in a wide swath of the rest of the world, Christians face active persecution—including physical abuse, eviction, exile, imprisonment, and even death—because of their faith. Some might assume that conditions have always been this bad, but in fact more Christians are under siege today for their faith than even during the Roman persecution of the Early Church.[99]

It is sad and very discouraging when persecution comes from within the faith community. For example, when Stephen stood up before the religious council and recapitulated the history of the Jewish people and how rebellious they have been toward the God of their salvation, and how their fathers persecuted all the prophets including Jesus Christ, the religious leaders and people were cut to their heart; and they stoned Stephen to death. (Acts 7:57-60) Persecution can come from those who attend church with you. When you stand up against wrong and injustice in your own church and in your denomination, be prepared to suffer persecution from those who value club-ship and membership more than discipleship. However, wherever persecution comes from, do not let it be a surprise to you. "Regardless, hostility should not come as a surprise. After all, our Lord warned in John 15:19, 'If you were of the world, the world would love you as its own; but because you are not of the world, but I chose you out of the world, therefore the world hates you.' Recall that our Lord came into this world to save it, knowing full well that He would encounter hostility that would climax at the cross. He chose us out of the world, yet leaves us here for a time as His ambassadors, knowing we will encounter hostility as we follow him."[100] Never forget that the world is in the church, and there are people who are

---

[99]Jesse Yow, Standing Firm A Christian Response To Hostility And Persecution, Published by Concordia Publishing House, 2015, 16-17.
[100] Ibid., 23.

in key positions that have never been born again spiritually. The reason it is so hard to advance the Kingdom of God in the church there are people who do not know Jesus, and want to use the church for their social strivings. They are like the Pharisees who "cleanse the outside of the cup and of the dish, but inside they are full of greediness and self-indulgence." (Matthew 23:25) Not having a relationship with Christ, they fight against the things that come from the Spirit of God . . . "is not able to understand them, because they are examined spiritually." (1 Corinthians 2:14) Instead of promoting the things that come through the Spirit, like blind Saul they persecute them and those who are carrying out the things of the Spirit.

So, before you plunge into despair being shocked that people in the church can be your greatest persecutors, take comfort in knowing that they are in the church but not of the church. Just like followers of Christ who are in the world but not of the world (John 17:16) So, don't do as many others are doing and make your faith a private matter due to the persecution you are receiving. Remember what Jesus told his followers centuries ago.

Jesus Begins Teaching on the Mountain

Matthew 5:1-12 Updated American Standard Version (UASV)

5 Having seen the crowds, he went up on the mountain;[101] and when he sat down, his disciples came to him. **2** And he opened his mouth and taught them, saying

Nine Beatitudes

3 "Blessed[102] are the poor[103] in spirit, for theirs is the kingdom of the heavens.

---

[101] Or *hill*

[102] I.e. fortunate or prosperous

⁴ "Blessed are those who mourn, for they shall be comforted.¹⁰⁴

⁵ "Blessed are the meek,¹⁰⁵ for they shall inherit the earth.

⁶ "Blessed are those who hunger and thirst for righteousness, for they shall be satisfied.

⁷ "Blessed are the merciful, for they shall receive mercy.

⁸ "Blessed are the pure in heart, for they shall see God.

⁹ "Blessed are the peacemakers, for they shall be called sons of God.

¹⁰ "Blessed are those who have been persecuted for the sake of righteousness, for theirs is the kingdom of the heavens.

¹¹ "Blessed are you when men reproach you and persecute you, and say all kinds of wicked thing against you falsely on account of me. ¹² Rejoice and be glad, for your reward in the heavens is great; for so they persecuted the prophets who were before you.

The more you become like Jesus, the more you will be a target for persecution; do not be ashamed to suffer for Jesus Christ.

When Paul and Silas were in Macedonia preaching Christ, Paul called a spirit of divination out of a young girl who was making money for her masters. When the masters saw that the young girl had lost her divination powers they went to

---

¹⁰³ "Blessed are those who [are poor in spirit] recognize they are spiritually helpless ..." (GOD'S WORD Translation) The Greek word *ptochos* means "beggar." The "poor in spirit" is an alternative literal rendering. The meaning is that the "beggar/poor in spirit" is aware of his or her spiritual needs, as if a beggar or the poor would be aware of their physical needs.

¹⁰⁴ Some ancient authorities transpose verses 4 and 5

¹⁰⁵ Or *gentle*

the magistrates of the city and had Paul and Silas beaten. Not only were these Christian men beaten but they were also thrown in jail because they countered a culture and its profit making schemes with the gospel of Jesus Christ. (Acts 16:16-24) Understand that persecution comes when you counter-cultural practices. Had Paul and Silas remained quiet about Christ and went along with whatever the culture was doing, they would have avoided persecution. Only when you decide to be a public witness for Christ do you experience persecution. "As long as a Christian is quiet about his or her faith in Christ, not saying anything to anyone about Christ, but praying and practicing faith in privacy, then that Christian faces far less risk of persecution. It is only when a Christian is public about his or her faith, applying faith in the public square and even proclaiming Christ, that persecution will inevitably occur."[106]

The reason culture is running morally amuck too many Christians are practicing a private Christianity. If you are silent about your faith in the marketplace, you love your life more than you love Jesus Christ. Jesus said, "The one who loves his soul[107] loses it, and the one who hates his soul[108] in this world will safeguard it for life eternal." (John 12:25) Nobody wants to be persecuted, but followers of Christ must understand that their faith is not to be privatized. They cannot be silent onlookers in the midst of wrong, evil, and injustice and say that they are Christians. The two are antithetical. You cannot be a follower of Jesus Christ and complacent, indolent, and practice social and political quietism. You cannot be a follower of Jesus Christ and water down his message to a

---

[106] David Platt, Counter Culture: A Compassionate Call to Counter Culture in a World of Poverty, Same-Sex Marriage, Racism, Sex Slavery, Immigration, Abortion, Persecution, Orphans and Pornography, Tyndale House Publishers, Inc., 2015, 233.

[107] I.e., *life*

[108] I.e., *life*

dying world. The church is guilty of watering down the gospel of Jesus Christ to keep the hounds of hell from attacking it. When Christians openly follow Christ, openly communicate his gospel, openly express his love and compassion, openly speak out against injustice and immorality, openly live a godly life, and openly do the will of God on earth as it is in heaven, Christians can expect openly that the world will automatically persecute them. Therefore, if you have privatized Christianity and walk around as a blindfold Christian not seeing the need to get involve to correct oppression, injustice, and help heal a broken world, you are not a follower of Jesus Christ. Jesus was very open with his faith, and he worked and spoke publicly about life issues that were out of line with the will of God. Followers of Christ are to do no less than Jesus did even though persecution comes as a result of public witness. You must remember that the goal is the win the world for Christ as did the early church won the Roman Empire for Christ. Melvin A. Hammarberg makes a very cogent point:

> First century Christianity was very costly, and it was not easy then to be a Christian. There was no light-hearted confidence in it, nor any sense of finding ease in the association. In that early day the Christian life was associated with effort and enterprise, with persecution, peril and tribulation. It tested powers of endurance. It confronted the perplexing problems. It challenged superior orders. It was tied to hard tasks, but the early Christians were committed and believed that their faith was indispensable to the redemption and well-being of mankind. The ills of mankind were ceaselessly and relentlessly to be attacked. Christian life was one of tremendous risk and danger. Here was a call and a challenge to live for, to fight for, and even to die for, as many did. It has a power of attraction that

captured heroic souls who were willing to try to conquer the world of that day.[109]

You cannot avoid persecution following Jesus Christ. Francis J. Grimke stated, "It takes courage to be a Christian; it takes courage to follow Jesus Christ. One of the most wonderful things to me in the early days of Christianity was the courage displayed by those early Christians—how in obedience to Jesus Christ they went forth into the midst of a hostile world, with public sentiment and everything against them; how in the face of danger, privation, suffering, and death, they held on uncompromisingly to Christian principles. They were willing to suffer, willing to be killed for them, but they were not willing to surrender them. So many of them suffered; many of them were martyred. And thus victory finally came."[110] Followers must engage their faith in the culture rather than hide it. To hide our faith is to be fearful of the consequences of making it public.

Some Christians have become ashamed of their faith hiding it so they will not be detected in certain places and around certain people. Jesus said, "Whoever is ashamed of me and of my words, of him will the Son of Man be ashamed when he comes in his glory and the glory of the Father and of the holy angels." (Luke 9:26) You cannot conquer what you refuse to face. Jesus faced the culture; he faced wrong, evil, and injustice; he faced name calling; he faced the false labels, and all the things that were thrown at him. Because he faced the culture and was open about his faith, Jesus transformed the culture through his followers who also endured the persecution, and finally turned the world right side up. So, when you suffer persecution for following Jesus

---

[109] Melvin A. Hammarberg, "To Dream The Impossible Dream" Augsburg Sermons, Series C,1973, Augsburg Publishing House, 232.

[110] Francis J. Grimke, "The Religious Aspect of Reconstruction (February 19, 1919), cited in The Faithful Preacher, by Thabitl M. Anyabwile, Crossway Books, Wheaton, Illinois, 2007, 166.

Christ, ponder on this insight from Dietrich Bonhoeffer. "Suffering, then, is the badge of true discipleship. The disciple is not above his master. Following Christ means passio passiva, suffering because we have to suffer. That is why Luther reckoned suffering among the marks of the true Church, and one of the memoranda drawn up in preparation for the Augsburg Confession similarly defines the Church as the community of those 'who are persecuted and martyred for the gospel's sake. . . Discipleship means allegiance to the suffering Christ, and it is therefore not at all surprising that Christians should be called upon to suffer."[111]

Always remember that suffering persecution for Christ is bringing others to the light. It is bringing redemption to a dark and lost world. Your persecution for Christ sake is not in vain. God through Christ used the persecution of the early Christians to bring many to the Christian faith. God wants to use your persecution to save others. Suffering persecution is a call that goes along with the good news of the gospel. It was stated that Christians in China underwent persecution but the church would not die. "The church went underground and grew. Groups of three and four began meeting in homes. Soon the numbers grew to 30, then to 50. They would sing, pray, study Bible passages carefully copied by hand and listen to a message from one of their own. Persecution helped create thousands of small, self-contained Christian communities which have operated in secret, mostly without ordained ministers—often, even without Bibles."[112]

Since, persecution is a definite reality for followers of Jesus Christ, the Apostle Paul tells us to "Put on the full armor of God, so that you will be able to stand firm against the schemes of the devil. For our wrestling[113] is not against flesh

---

[111] Dietrich Bonhoeffer, The Cost of Discipleship, Collier Books Macmillan Publishing Company, 1963, 100-101.

[112] Colleen Townsend Evans, The Vine Life, 120.

[113] Or struggle

and blood, but against the rulers, against the powers, against the world-rulers of this darkness, against the wicked spirit forces in the heavenly places. Therefore, take up the whole armor[114] of God, so that you will be able to resist in the evil day, and having done everything, to stand firm." (Ephesians 6:11-13) We must keep the armor of the Lord on at all times. Tony Evans said, "Our problem today is that we have too many Christian civilians and not enough Christian soldiers. Some of us simply want to jump into a soldier's uniform when we run into a problem, rather than understanding we are soldiers who are supposed to be in uniform at all times because we are in a war."[115]

Paul knew the world would reject Jesus Christ and that his followers would face persecution again and again. Right now there are Christians being persecuted in other parts of the world for their Christian faith. In America Christians are blessed to have laws in place to protect religious freedom. However, in time Christians in America must face the fact that their faith also will come under attack. There are glimpses of this already taking place in the land. Regardless of how much religious freedom Christians have today in America, it will soon be attacked and Christians must match their faith with their confession. Lip service won't cut it anymore. Christians must be willing to suffer in whatever form it comes to demonstrate that their faith is more than mere confession. Like Daniel, the three Hebrew men, and

---

[114] **Armor:** (Heb. *keli*; Gr. *panoplia*) The weapons and armor worn by soldiers used in fighting, which makes up the whole of his offensive and defensive equipment. This would include a helmet to protect the head, the girdle, and a leather belt worn around the waist or hips to protect the loins, the breastplate to protect vital organs, especially the heart. It also included a coat of mail, i.e., scale body armor for protection during battle, greaves, namely shin guards, and the shield, usually carried on the left arm or in the left hand.–1 Sam. 7:5-6; 31:9; Eph. 6:13-17.

[115] Tony Evans, Speaks Out On Spiritual Warfare, Moody Press, 2000, 52.

many others demonstrated by their refusal to surrender their faith and principles to majority opinion, and willing to lose everything in including their lives for the Kingdom of God, followers of Christ today are expected to do no less. In other words, count on suffering persecution as a follower of Jesus Christ. It will and must happen due to the value conflict of the Kingdom of this world and the Kingdom of God.

"However, Christians should not panic. For two thousand years, this has been what it has meant to identify with Christ in the world—the normal experience of those who followed a man who was crucified. Suffering for the gospel was not just tolerated in the early church; it was expected. . . . Soon enough, though the expectation of American Christians will necessarily adjust to what is normal for the true church in other times and places. We will increasingly realize that when we proclaim a gospel like ours and make the sorts of claims we do, the world won't typically receive it well. For Christians, it really is strange not to be persecuted."[116] Tony Evans says, "Let's face it. The cross does involve suffering. It's an instrument of death. Bearing my cross means I am willing to identify publicly with Jesus Christ and accept anything that goes with that identification. It means I will bear the scars of being identified with Christ. But the cross is also the path to resurrection glory."[117] Therefore, don't be surprised when you are persecuted for Jesus Christ! It may be hard to do but "Rejoice and be glad, for your reward in the heavens is great; for so they persecuted the prophets who were before you." (Matthew 5:12) When times are really hard and trying for you, here is a hymn to help you cope with suffering persecution on your journey with Christ!

What a Friend we have in Jesus,
   All our sins and griefs to bear!

---

[116] John Piper & David Mathis, Think It Not Strange Navigating Trials In The New America, Published by Desiring God, 2016, 6-7.
[117] Tony Evans, Speaks Out On Spiritual Warfare, 27.

What a privilege to carry
　Everything to God in prayer!
O what peace we often forfeit,
　O what needless pain we bear,
All because we do not carry
　Everything to God in prayer!

Have we trials and temptations?
　Is there trouble anywhere?
We should never be discouraged,
　Take it to the Lord in prayer.
Can we find a friend so faithful
　Who will all our sorrows share?
Jesus knows our every weakness,
　Take it to the Lord in prayer.
Are we weak and heavy-laden,
　Cumbered with a load of care?
Precious Savior, still our refuge—
　Take it to the Lord in prayer;
Do thy friends despise, forsake thee?
　Take it to the Lord in prayer;
In His arms He'll take and shield thee,
　Thou wilt find a solace there.[118]

[118] Joseph M. Scriven, 1819-1866, "What A Friend We Have In Jesus"
Tune: Annie Lowery, 8787 D, Traditional Celtic; arr. Valeria A. Foster,
2000, GIA Publication, Inc.

CHAPTER EIGHT Expect Death

Acts 7:59-60 Updated American Standard Version (UASV)

⁵⁹ And as they were stoning Stephen, he called out, "Lord Jesus, receive my spirit." ⁶⁰ Then falling on his knees, he cried out with a loud voice, "Lord, do not hold this sin against them!" Having said this, he fell asleep.[119]

It is well documented the many souls that were kill for daring to believe in Jesus Christ and confronting the world with his gospel. The early Christian movement was a real movement that did not start in a classroom; it wasn't the results of an intellectual conference on religion; it didn't start in the church or temple. It started from among the common people who heard Jesus gladly (Mark 12:35-37) and as a result of hearing and following Jesus; they paid a heavy price. They were willing to die because Jesus had made such an impact upon their hearts, minds, and souls that they were willing to lay down their lives for his cause. They were willing to give up everything, life, security, comfort, position, etc. to be living sacrifices for him whom they believed to be the Son of God. Many of them lost their lives for following him. Not all of them were martyred, but they were willing and ready to pay the cost for following the man from Galilee. Whenever Christians get over the fear of death, they are free to do God's will no matter the cost. The Apostle Paul said, "For to me to live is Christ, and to die is gain." (Philippians 1:21) Paul and the early Christians had the conviction that Jesus Christ alone is worth living for and worth dying for. Since, death has no sting and no victory, and cannot separate us from the love of God, which is in Christ Jesus our Lord, why flinch when facing death when

---

[119] I.e. died

Jesus has already declared, "I am the resurrection and the life. The one trusting in me, though he dies, yet shall he live, and everyone living and trusting in me shall never die. Do you trust this?" (John 11:25-26) Having this faith conviction in their hearts, the early apostles and Christians surrendered their lives for Jesus Christ.

In both the Old and New Testament we find people who were martyrs for their faith. Over the centuries millions of God's people have been killed due to their faith. To name a few examples are the following. Cain killed his brother Abel. (Genesis 4:8) Zechariah was stoned to death at the commandment of the king in the court of the house of the LORD. (2 Chronicles 24:21) Attempted murder was practiced on Daniel and three Hebrew men (Daniel 3:20, 6:16). John the Baptist was beheaded in prison, (Mark 6:27). Stephen was stoned to death. (Acts 7:57-58) James, the apostle, was also killed. (Acts 12:2) It was predicted that Peter would be killed. (John 21:18-19) Other sources believe Peter was crucified upside down. The Romans beheaded the Apostle Paul. These are just a few examples of the many people who lost their lives for their faith. We cannot deny the fact that death is a certainty when you decide to live out the faith in this mean, evil, and ungodly world.

God's people suffered and died for the faith in the past, and today, Christian followers of Christ must be willing to do the same. Postmodern times don't erase the call nor the commitment to do as God's people have done in the past. Followers of Christ today are expected to follow suit with a great number of previous followers who met the demands of discipleship. Therefore, without mincing words and being hyperbole, on this journey with Jesus Christ, you must face the fact of the definiteness of physical death. As it was stated earlier, at all times, you must be cemetery ready to lay down your life for Jesus Christ. In giving your life, you are making a statement to the world that not even death will cause you to denounce the Lordship of Jesus Christ. Those who did not

111

allow the fear of death to arrest their work and commitment to God are the ones you should look to for encouragement and inspiration. Often times the threat of death is used as a deterrent to doing the will of God. As long as followers of Jesus Christ are fearful, they cannot be faithful to the Lord's call. However, when death is no longer a fear for God's people, they are free to do His will and serve His cause.

For example, when Moses was no longer fearful of going back to Egypt, he was able to stand before Pharaoh and say, "'Thus says Jehovah, 'Let my people go, that they may serve me.'" (Exodus 8:1) Facing the death of the fiery furnace, three Hebrew men refused to bow to the golden image King Nebuchadnezzar set up. (Daniel 3:16-18) Daniel knew King Darius enacted a new law, and anybody who disobeyed would be thrown into the den of lions. However, Daniel continued to pray three times and gave thanks to God as was his customs (Daniel 6:10). Esther knew that anyone who goes into the inner court without permission could be put to death. But, she decided to go anyhow and said, "If I perish, I perish." (Esther 4:11-16) Each one of these biblical stories along with much more shows that God's people cannot allow the threat of death to cause them to recant their faith and work for the Lord. Regardless of the threat of death, when God's people allow themselves to be used by God, God can get the victory and the glory. Death should not be feared when we believe it is the door to eternal life.

Followers of Jesus Christ must be courageous and never afraid to give up this temporary life. The God we trust with this life can be trusted on through to the next life. David speaks for all followers of God through Christ when facing death. Even though I walk through the valley of the shadow of death, I will fear no evil, for you are with me; your rod and your staff, they comfort me." (Psalm 23:4) No one who followers Jesus Christ should be afraid to let go of this physical life and come alive in Jesus Christ. When followers have died to themselves, they can stand against any power

112

and authority and say and do what God is calling them to do. For example, when a reformer named John Huss refused to make the claim that the pope is the head of the church, Huss and other reformers lost their lives for teaching and believing that only Christ is the Head of the Church. When the Roman Catholic Church arrested him and gave him another chance to recant, he refused and they burned him alive. He and the other reformers were cemetery ready to give up their lives for Jesus Christ. While dying, Huss said, "Lord Jesus, it is for thee that I patiently endure this cruel death. I pray thee to have mercy on my enemies."[120] Huss spoke similar words Stephen spoke while dying for Jesus Christ. "Lord, do not hold this sin against them!" (Acts 7:60) Don Benton stated, "Stephen was one who had taken the words of Jesus seriously. He counted the cost and decided to continue to follow. Stephen was the first Christian martyr because he determined that he would rather die for his faith than deny it. They stoned Stephen primarily because he was attacking the root causes of evil and oppression in his day as his master had done."[121]

As a follower of Christ, you cannot allow death to paralyze you. In the Columbine High School massacre in 1999, a young 17-year-old girl named Cassie Rene Bernall was asked by the shooter "Does she believe in God." It is reported that she said "YES" and the shooter took her life. Cassie like many martyrs before her did not deny the faith while staring death in the face. They must have believed with their whole heart "Absent from the body present with the Lord (2 Corinthians 5:8)." Therefore, followers of Christ must remember that they are involved in a spiritual warfare of which their participation and courage are essential for the task. So, if you truly love God and His Son Jesus Christ, count

---

[120] Cited in 131 Christians Everyone Should Know by Mark Galli and Ted Olsen, Broadman & Holman Publishers, 2000, 369-71.

[121] Don Benton, The Cost of Being Christian, C.S.S. Publishing Company, 1989, 87.

the cost for this love. It cost Stephen and many more their lives. If you are willing to pay the price, then let go the fear of death because "There is no fear in love; but perfect love casts out fear, because fear has to do with punishment,[122] and the one who fears is not perfected in love." (1 John 4:18)

Like soldiers who are deployed to go to war must be prepared to lay down his life as a consequence of war. So, it is with Christian disciples. Those who follow Jesus Christ into spiritual combat must be prepared to not only win some victories but suffer some losses as well. The losses on earth are really gains of eternal life for the Kingdom of God. Paul said, "For to me to live is Christ, and to die is gain." (Philippians 1:21) Therefore, if you are afraid to die, you cannot be a disciple of Jesus Christ. Dietrich Bonhoeffer makes it plain. "When Christ calls a man, he bids him to come and die. It may be a death like that of the first disciples who had to leave home and work to follow him, or it may be a death like Luther's who had to leave the monastery and go out into the world. But it is the same death every time— death in Jesus Christ, the death of the old man at his call."[123] Jesus never taught or demonstrated that disciples should avoid death or compromise in such a way to escape death. Christ calls disciples to face and accept the inevitability of death. Jesus said, "For whoever would save his soul[124] will lose it, but whoever loses his soul[125] for my sake will find it." (Matthew 16:25) Followers or disciples of Christ must understand, "If we lose our lives in his service and carry our cross, we shall find our lives again in the fellowship of the

---

[122] Gr., Kolasin (Lit., lopping off cutting off), the punishment is the fear of being cut off, i.e., not remaining in God's love on judgment day.

[123] Dietrich Bonhoeffer, The Cost of Discipleship, Collier Books Macmillan Publishing Company, 1963, 99.

[124] I.e., life

[125] I.e., life

cross with Christ."[126] Dying is not something we look forward to and relish in, but as a disciple of Jesus Christ you must be willing to lay your life down in order to take up eternal life. As Jesus laid down his life for our salvation, you must be willing to lay down your life for Christ and the gospel he brought us.

The reason culture is spiritually untransformed too many Christians fear death. The threat of death has caused many Christians to recant their efforts to win the culture of Christ, and as a result, the moral toxicity of the land is reaching new lows. While church edifices are more grander than ever before, while there is an increase in religious conferences taking place across the nation, while more Christian television stations are being added, Christianity is not only dwindling, it is losing the cultural war and losing souls for the Kingdom of God. Too many Christians, especially in America, are acting like the pre-Pentecost disciples who were behind closed doors fearful of bringing to bear the gospel of Jesus Christ on the culture. Fear paralyzed them; it immobilized them because they were afraid to die for Jesus Christ. They hid, and a few wanted to go back to their previous occupations. They met in secret to discuss Jesus. They had done what so many Christians are doing today privatized their faith.

However, something amazingly happened. When they were in the upper room, the Holy Spirit came upon them like a mighty rushing wind, and they were all filled with the Holy Spirit. (Acts 2:1-4) After this Pentecost experience, we see the boldness of the disciples and their impact on the world. Since they were now filled with the Holy Spirit, the fear of death no longer held them captive. They boldly witnessed for Christ in the marketplaces not fearing the consequences for their boldness. When followers of Christ are filled with the Holy Spirit, they can master their fear. When facing death while doing the will of God, the Holy Spirit brings back to

---

[126] Ibid., 101.

remembrance the consoling words of Jesus. "Do not be afraid of those who kill the body but cannot kill the soul. Rather, be afraid of the One who can destroy soul and body in hell (Matthew 10:28)." Only when followers of Christ are filled with the Holy Spirit can they do the will of God in spite of the fear of death or nonbeing. The Holy Spirit helps the follower of Christ to be bold and unrelenting.

Therefore, followers of Christ must remember that "For God did not give us a spirit of cowardice, but one of power and of love and of soundness of mind."[127] (2 Timothy 1:7) Since God is not the giver of fear, it must come from the enemy of God, Satan, the devil who desires to arrest the influence of the gospel of Jesus Christ in the world. Christians today must understand that they must expect death but should not fear death. Christ has conquered death. While following Christ in this immorally sick world, Martin Luther King, Jr. reminds us "It may even mean physical death. However, if physical death is the price that [Christians] must pay to free [their children] and [their brothers and sisters] from a permanent death of the spirit, then nothing could be more redemptive. This is the type of soul force that I am convinced will triumph over the physical force of the oppressor."[128]

Bonhoeffer speaks to followers of Christ as well. He said, "They must not fear men. Men can do them no harm, for the power of men ceases with the death of the body. But they must overcome the fear of death with the fear of God. The

---

[127] **Sound in Mind**: (Gr. *sophroneo*) This means to be of sound mind or in one's right mind, i.e., to have understanding about practical matters and thus be able to act sensibly, 'to have sound judgment, to be sensible, to use good sense, sound judgment.'—Acts 26:25; Romans 12:3; 2 Timothy 1:7; Titus 2:6; 1 Peter 4:7

[128] Martin Luther King, Jr., A Testament Of Hope The Essential Writings of Martin Luther King, Jr. Edited by James Melvin Washington, Harper & Row, Publishers, 1986, 149.

danger lies not in the judgement of men, but in the judgement of God, not in the death of the body, but in the external destruction of body and soul. Those who are still afraid of men have no fear of God, and those who have fear of God have ceased to be afraid of men. All preachers of the gospel will do well to recollect this saying daily."[129] Therefore, there should be no hesitation to do God's will when faced with the possibility of physical death. When you know that God can destroy both body and soul, God is the One you should ultimately fear. Don't fear people; people are limited in what they can do to you. People can destroy the body but this is all they can do. They cannot do anymore. So, don't let the fear of death paralyze you to the point you are frozen in intimidation. Paul Borthwick stated, "If the fear of death paralyzes us, we will never venture into the poor places, the violent places and the dangerous places of the world—the places that are most lacking in the knowledge of the good news of Jesus Christ. Without risk-takers with eternity in their hearts, who will reach the gangs of the cities, the improvised, those dying of AIDs, the terrorists? . . . Involvement in the global enterprise of following Christ requires death in various shapes and sizes. Some will literally be asked to die (John 12:24), while others will be asked to die to selfishness, materialism, consumerism and all the other enemies of the Jesus-exalting gospel."[130]

Needless to say that no war can be won if soldiers are frozen in fear. Since, followers of Christ are in a spiritual warfare, they cannot allow themselves to be afraid to die. Like in any war, there will be causalities. In addition, if you are a causality, remember good wine comes from crushed grapes. Since, Jesus is the true vine, and we the branches that abide in him, fruit come from this connection. When the

---

[129] Dietrich Bonhoeffer, The Cost of Discipleship, 242.
[130] Paul Borthwick, Six Dangerous Questions to transform your view of the world, InterVarity Press, 1996, 62-63.

grapes on the vine are ready to be transformed into something else, the grapes are crushed, but what comes forth is a new reality. The point is when it is time for you to die or be crushed for Jesus sake, you become fresh wine in the Kingdom of God. You take on a new reality. Death on this side of time has transformed you into life on the other side of eternity. There is no reason to allow the expectation of death as a follower of Jesus Christ to stop you from doing his will on earth. This is the reason the early Christians were willing to die because they believed that there is life in Christ beyond physical death. "When persecution came to the Christian church during the heady days of the Roman Empire, the believers realized that the pagans could take many things from them: wealth, food, friends and health, to name a few. But they could not rid Christians of the gift of death that would escort them into the presence of God. Indeed, God often used the pagans to give His children that special present without no man can see the Lord."[131] If more Christians were not afraid of death, more could get done for the Kingdom of God. But, due to the fact that many Christians are afraid to die, this fear is a weapon Satan, the devil uses to keep Christians from acting on behalf of the Kingdom of God. It keeps the church frozen in complacency and embracing the status quo.

Followers must understand that Jesus gave his life for the church. He did not want to die, but he gave up his will for his Father's will. "And going a little farther he fell on his face and prayed, saying, 'My Father, if it be possible, let this cup pass from me; yet not as I will, but as you will.'" (Matthew 26:39) Notice here that it says Jesus "went a little farther." This is an example for followers of Jesus Christ. They must go a little farther. When opposition, criticism, loneliness, temptation, misunderstanding, the threat of death, and the

---

[131] Erwin W. Lutzer, One Minute After You Die, Moody Publishers, 2015, 62.

fiery darts of the devil are launched against them, they must give up their will for the will of God and go a little farther. Although this is hard and keeps followers unnerved, death should not intimidate to the point that followers are fearful of losing their lives when they stand against Satan and his Kingdom. This is the reason the Apostle Paul was inspired to write, "For I am convinced that neither death, nor life, nor angels, nor rulers, nor things present, nor things to come, nor powers, nor height, nor depth, nor any other created thing, will be able to separate us from the love of God that is in Christ Jesus our Lord." (Romans 8:38-39) Paul encapsulates whatever followers go through or have to face there isn't anything on this planet that can separate them from the love of God, which is in Christ Jesus our Lord.

So when you are persecuted for righteousness, stand up against social and economic practices that are out of line with the will of God, advocate for the poor and the oppressed, plead for the needy, speak out against injustice and a sexually immoral culture, danger and death will stare you in the face. At the same time, eternal life and the Kingdom of God are waiting to receive you should your physical life be taken for righteousness sake. Please understand that as a follower of Jesus Christ, your home is not this world. You are a pilgrim traveling through to enter the Kingdom of God that cannot be moved. Therefore, expect death but don't fear it. "Death is inevitable. . . . The God who brought our whirling planet from primal vapor and has led the human pilgrimage for these many centuries can most assuredly lead us through death's dark night into the bright daybreak of eternal life. His will is too perfect, and his purposes are too extensive to be contained in the limited receptacle of time and the narrow walls of earth. Death is not the ultimate evil; the ultimate evil is to be outside of God's love."[132] If more Christians truly believed "Absent from the body present with Lord," they

---

[132] Martin Luther King, Jr., Strength to Love, Fortress Press, 1963, 124.

would take more risk for the Kingdom of God. They would be a voice for righteousness not an echo of the status quo; they would stand and declare without the fear of death and say to the empires of the world, "If this be so, our God whom we serve is able to deliver us from the burning fiery furnace, and he will deliver us out of your hand, O king. But if not, be it known to you, O king, that we will not serve your gods or worship the golden image that you have set up." (Daniel 3:17-18) Followers of Christ have to expect death, but they can also expect that the Savior of life is with them and will never leave them alone. Jesus said, "I am with you always, even to the end of the age." (Matthew 28:20) There is not a day, an hour, nor a minute that the Savior is not with the followers. Whatever crisis, whatever situation, whatever circumstances followers find themselves in, they can be assured that the presence of the Lord is with them. Because the Lord of life is always with His people, "Think of how powerless death actually is! Rather than rid us of our wealth, it introduces us to 'riches eternal.' In exchange for poor health, death gives us a right to the Tree of Life that is for 'the healing of the nations.' (Revelations 22:2) Death might temporarily take our friends from us, but only to introduce us to that land in which there are no good-byes."[133] The following hymn by Thomas Andrew Dorsey can help you face death and strengthen your heart and your faith. It is called "Precious Lord, Take My Hand."

Precious Lord, take my hand,
Lead me on, let me stand,
I am tired, I am weak, I am worn;
Through the storm, through the night,
Lead me on to the light:

Refrain

Take my hand, precious Lord,

---

[133] Erwin W. Lutzer, One Minute After You Die, 62.

Lead me home.
When my way grows drear,
Precious Lord, linger near,
When my life is almost gone,
Hear my cry, hear my call,
Hold my hand lest I fall:

Refrain

Take my hand, precious Lord,
Lead me home.
When the darkness appears
And the night draws near,
And the day is past and gone,
At the river I stand,
Guide my feet, hold my hand:

Refrain

Take my hand, precious Lord,
Lead me home.[134]

---

[134] Thomas A. Dorsey, "Precious Lord Take My Hand," 1932, ©
1938, Unichappell Music, Inc. (renewed). Assigned to Warner-Tamerlane
Publishing Corp.

CHAPTER NINE The Great Reward

Matthew 25:21 Updated American Standard Version (UASV)

²¹ His master said to him: 'Well done, good and faithful slave! You were faithful over a few things. I will appoint you over many things. Enter into the joy of your master.'

There is nothing like hearing the words of the Savior to the faithful servant, "Well Done. . . . Enter into the joy of your Lord." Out of all the words we have heard in life, these words spoken by Jesus to his servants are like great costly pearls. Being eternally in the joy of the Lord trumps everything servants went through on earth for the cause of Christ. As the Apostle Paul stated, "For our affliction is momentary and light, it is producing for us an eternal weight of glory far beyond all comparison" (2 Corinthians 4:17) The glory of being with the Lord cannot be compared to anything on earth. The most beautiful places on earth are incomparable to the glory of being with the Lord. If you have visited the White House in America, Buckingham Palace in London, Alcazar of Seville in Spain, the Grand Palace of Bangkok, the Kremlin of Moscow, and the most exotic places on earth these cannot compare to the glory of being with the Lord.

Those who followed Christ and remained faithful despite being persecuted and killed have something great to look forward to. Jesus said, "Rejoice and be glad, for your reward in the heavens is great; for so they persecuted the prophets who were before you." (Matthew 5:12) The reward is of such greatness it cannot be adequately described. No wonder Paul declared, "Eye has not seen, and ear has not heard, and have not entered into the heart of man, all that God has prepared for those who love him." (1 Corinthians 2:9) What is in store for the faithful servants of Christ is so unlike anything they have experienced on earth. It is an understatement to try to describe it. No one can describe spiritual, eternal rewards in physical terms. It is just impossible to do.

Therefore, when the eschatological judgment comes, followers of Christ do not have to worry because "For the Lord himself will descend from heaven with a cry of command, with the voice of an archangel, and with the sound of the trumpet of God, and the dead in Christ will rise first. Then we who are alive, who remain will be caught up together with them in the clouds to meet the Lord in the air, and so we shall always be with the Lord." (1 Thessalonians 4:16-17) Regardless of the cosmic catalytic occurrences taking place in the universe and on the earth upon the Lord's arrival, followers of Christ do not have to fret or be afraid because they shall always be with the Lord. According to Scripture, "But the day of the Lord will come like a thief, in which the heavens will pass away with a loud noise, the elements will burn and be dissolved, and the earth and its works will be exposed.[135] (2 Peter 3:10)

Think about it all the silver, gold, and economies of this world that people have given their lives to possess and never laid up any treasure in heaven shall pass away with fervent heat. Think about all the billionaires who spent a lifetime storing up treasure on earth but were never rich toward God shall have it all pass away. Think about all oppressors who exploited the oppressed and crushed the poor to have a life of ease, comfort, and luxury on earth and never repented of their sins shall have it all go up in smoke. Only what we have done for Christ shall have eternal rewards. Treasure laid up in heaven far exceeds any treasure on earth. Jesus said, "For where your treasure is, there your heart will be also."

------

[135] Gr *heurethesetai* ("will be discovered") is attested to by אּ B KP 424ᶜ 1175 1739ᵗˣᵗ 1852 syrᵖʰ, ʰᵐᵍ ᵃʳᵐ Origen. Gr *katakaesetai* ("will be burned up") is attested to by A 048 049 056 0142 33 614 Byz Lect syrʰ copᵇᵒ eth *al.*

123

(Matthew 6:21) Because followers of Christ kept the connection between the vertical and the horizontal, and their hearts were heavenward and they used their treasure to serve Christ on earth, they have treasure in heaven stored up for their arrival. What treasure on earth can top being "Heirs of God, and joint-heirs with Christ?" What investments on earth can have greater returns than being victorious with Jesus Christ? These laid up treasures won't rust or be stolen because criminality is nonexistent in the Kingdom of God.

In the final spiritual battle against Satan, the faithful are victorious. The saints overcame Satan. "And they conquered him because of the blood of the Lamb and because of the word of their witnessing, and they did not love their souls even in death." (Revelation 12:11) Regardless how much they suffered, the agony of their affliction, the pain they endured, the rejection, criticism, persecution, and the starless midnights they had to withstand for the gospel of Jesus Christ, they are now victorious. "Those who rule with Christ are overcomers, those who have successfully conquered the challenges of this life. They have weathered the storms and have believed in God's promises against incredible odds. They have willingly suffered for His name. They have resisted the threefold seduction of pleasure, possessions, and power."[136] The great day of the Lord has come, and the separation of the sheep from the goats is at hand. "'Then the King will say to those on his right: 'Come, you who have been blessed by my Father, inherit the Kingdom prepared for you from the founding of the world. For I became hungry, and you gave me something to eat; I was thirsty, and you gave me something to drink. I was a stranger and you received me hospitably; naked and you clothed me. I fell sick and you looked after me. I was in prison and you visited me.' ... In reply the King will say to them, 'Truly I say to you, to the

---

[136] Erwin Lutzer, Your Eternal Reward, Triumph and Tears at the Judgment Seat of Christ, Moody Publishers, 2015, 137-138.

extent that you did it to one of the least of these my brothers, you did it to me.'" (Matthew 25:34-36, 40) Eternal compensation for following and serving Christ is the great reward for the saints.

Sacrifices for the Kingdom

Matthew 19:27-29 Updated American Standard Version (UASV)

²⁷ Then Peter said to him, "Look, we have left everything and followed you; what then will there be for us?" ²⁸ Jesus said to them: "Truly I say to you, in the renewal,[137] when the Son of man sits down on his glorious throne, you who have followed me will sit on twelve thrones, judging the twelve tribes of Israel.[138] ²⁹ And everyone who has left houses or brothers or sisters or father or mother or children or lands, for the sake of my name will receive a hundred times as much, and will inherit eternal life.

---

[137] **Recreation**: (Gr., *palingenesiai*) (*palin*, "again," plus *genao*, "to give birth") This is a period in which the already existing world (earth) and soul (person) begins anew, starting over, being refashioned into God's originally intended purpose. This is a renewal of the world during the second coming of Christ, after abyssing Satan and the demons, bringing in a new age that will restore the earth to its original purpose.– Dan. 7:13-14; Rev. 3:21; 20:1-6.

[138] **19:28 BDC: How are we to understand "the twelve tribes of Israel" that will be judged?** Jesus was speaking to the apostles, who are a part of "the [spiritual] Israel of God." (Gal. 6:16) This "twelve tribes of Israel" are not part of the spiritual Israel of God. Jesus made 'a covenant with them [spiritual Israel] for a kingdom,' and they were to be 'a kingdom and priests to our God.' (Luke 22:28-30; Rev. 5:10) These "holy ones" of spiritual Israel are to "judge the world." (1 Cor. 6:2) Therefore, "the twelve tribes of Israel," being spoken of here is pictorial of God's people as a whole after Armageddon, when Satan has been abyssed, and the kingdom of God is judging during a new age, the millennial reign, that will restore the earth and God's people to his original purpose.

Jesus, who is never out of touch with our fears, frustrations, and dilemmas, understands our human concerns. He understands that it is a lot to ask people to follow him; he understands it is a lot to ask people to deny themselves and pick up the cross and follow him daily. He understands it is a lot to ask people to love their enemies, bless them that curse you, and do good to them that hate you, and pray for them that despitefully use and persecute you. He understands it is a lot to ask people to step out of their sense of security into apparent insecurity. Jesus understands his spiritual demands on us.

To hear the words of the Savior "Well Done! Come, you blessed of My Father, inherit the Kingdom" is the promise made good in heaven; it is the great return on the great investment. The faithful servants who hear these words will know that when they served and met the needs of others, they were actually serving and meeting the needs of the Savior. When nobody saw them serving in secret, the Lord saw it and now rewards them openly. For their service to others, they shall inherit the Kingdom of God. "The great and unspeakable reward and honor that will be bestowed and conferred on the faithful servants of Christ will be a matter of great joy. It will exhibit the condescending grace of God and excite humility in them; they will scarcely believe that God could ever take notice and reward such poor services as they have done."[139] The compensation received far exceeds the committed service rendered. The saints are forever humbled and joyful for such great reward in comparison to such small service rendered. The following words of Lemuel Hayes should encourage the saints not to give up serving Christ on earth because of the great reward that awaits them:

---

[139] Lemuel Hayes, "The Suffering, Support, and Reward of Faithful Ministers, Cited in The faithful Preacher, THABITI M. ANYABWILE, Crossway Books, 2007, 61.

As God's rewarding the saints will humble them, so it will tend to fit them for the world of everlasting adoration. One great design of the day of judgment will be to exhibit the riches of divine grace, which will excite endless songs of joy to the saints. . . . God will make it evident that those who had trials of cruel mocking and scourging, of bonds and imprisonments, who were stoned and sawn asunder, tempted, slain with the sword, who wandered about in sheepskins and goatskins, in deserts, on mountains, and in dens and caves of the earth, being destitute, afflicted, tormented, were [people], after all, 'of whom the world was not worthy' (Heb. 11:36-38). The scars and signs of suffering in the cause of God that His people will carry with them will procure more illustrious monuments than pillars of marble. They will possess the Kingdom prepared for them and will be made Kings and priests unto God.[140]

People of every description, nation, and tongue shall enter God's Kingdom where there is endless peace, joy, and happiness. There won't any need for documentation, visas, or citizenship verification. Washed by blood of Christ is all that is needed, and reward for the faithful service rendered is now at hand. Though countless people will share in this endless joyful experience, every saint will be personally known by the Lord. No one will be lost in the crowd nor work forgotten on behalf of the cause of Jesus Christ. The Lord does not suffers from amnesia. The Hebrew writer states, "For God is not unjust so as to overlook your work and the love that you have shown for his name in serving the holy ones, as you still do." (Hebrews 6:10) A saint's individual life, sacrifice, and faithfulness will not go unnoticed and never forgotten. The Apostle Paul said, "Henceforth there is laid up for me the crown of righteousness, which the Lord, the

---

[140] Ibid., 61-62.

righteous judge, will award to me on that day, and not only to me but also to all who have loved his appearing." (2 Timothy 4:8) There are five types of crowns: the crown of righteousness (2 Timothy 4:7-8); imperishable crown (1 Corinthians 9:24-27); the crown of life (Revelation 2:10); the crown of rejoicing (1 Thessalonians 2:19-20); the crown of glory (1 Peter 5:1-4). Whichever crown a saint is given, it will fit the saint's individual life and head, and Christ will know the saint individually. Just like an earthy family, regardless of the number of children born or adopted in a family, parents know each of them individually. A saint will be known individually by God and Jesus Christ. As God "Counts the number of the stars; He calls them all by name (Psalms 147:4)," a saint will be given special individual attention. Again, the author of Hebrews says, "For God is not unjust so as to overlook your work and the love that you have shown for his name in serving the holy ones, as you still do." (Hebrews 6:10) The saints shall take part of the praise and worship of the King of Kings and Lord of Lords for doing for them what they could not do for themselves. Christ is worthy to be praised for giving His life for the sins of the world and making it possible for the saints to experience salvation.

Not only will crowns be given out to the saints, but they will be so overjoyed they cannot stop their tears of joy. If God did not wipe away the tears of the saints, they would perpetually cry when they see how blessed and undeserving they are of God's goodness. Erwin Lutzer stated, "When we reflect on how we lived for Christ, who purchased us at such high cost, well might we weep on the other side of the celestial gates. Our tears will be those of regret and shame, tears of remorse for lives lived for ourselves rather than for Him who 'loves us and released us from our sins by His blood' (Revelation 1:5 NASB). Perhaps we would never cease crying in heaven if God Himself did not come and wipe the tears from our eyes (Revelation 21:4)."[141] When the saints reflect on God's goodness and how they made it to the Kingdom of God despite their character defects, they cannot help but cry tears of joy for a kind and gracious God who looked beyond their faults and saw their need. However, crying cannot take place long for God shall wipe away their tears. Not only will there be anymore crying, "and death shall be no more, neither shall there be mourning, nor crying, nor pain anymore, for the former things, have passed away." (Revelation 21:4) When you think of what the saints had to go through on earth, it pales in comparison what is stored up for them.

Imagine the state of mind the saints will be in. Think of the joy, happiness, and jubilation you feel when your team wins the final competition. All of the practice, the hard work, and the sacrifice that went into winning, and at times it looked like the team is losing and the clock is running out of time; but just before the clock ticks out, the team wins. What joy! What jubilation and inspiration you feel when your team secures the victory! Despite the opposition against the team; despite the fumbles, mistakes, and fouls that the team made, it pales in comparison when the team prevails as the winner. The point here is it looks like following Jesus Christ is a losing battle; it seems living the Christian life is a waste of time; it looks like being a disciple in an ungodly culture is of no benefit. With all of the scandals, fumbles, fouls, accusations, persecutions, suffering, and misunderstanding that were part of the battle between followers and the world, in the end, Christ's team wins. His disciples are victorious. They overcame the opposition against them. They now shall inherit the Kingdom of God. Their great reward is eternal life. There is not anything greater to have bestowed on saints than eternal life with God and Jesus Christ.

---

[141] Erwin W. Lutzer, Your Eternal Reward Triumph and Tears at the Judgment Seat of Christ, Moody Publishers, 2015, 9-10.

The Scriptures only give us a glimpse of what our inheritance is with God and Jesus Christ. Isaiah the prophet describes our eternal dwelling in utopian terms of which there is universal peace. There won't be such things as war and conflict, predator and prey in the Kingdom of God. All inhabitants of the Kingdom of God shall have a new nature including the animals.

Isaiah 11:6-9 Updated American Standard Version (UASV)

⁶ The wolf will dwell with the lamb,
   and the leopard will lie down with the young goat,
and the calf and the lion and the fattened calf together;
   and a little boy will lead them.
⁷ The cow and the bear will graze;
   their young will lie down together;
   and the lion will eat straw like the ox.
⁸ The nursing child will play over the hole of the cobra,
   and the weaned child will put his hand on the adder's den.
⁹ They shall not hurt or destroy
   in all my holy mountain;
for the earth shall be full of the knowledge of Jehovah
   as the waters cover the sea.

The prophet Micah advances the utopian reality and further said,

Micah 4:3-4 Updated American Standard Version (UASV)

³ He shall judge between many peoples,
   and shall decide for strong nations far away;
and they shall beat their swords into plowshares,
   and their spears into pruning hooks;
nation shall not lift up sword against nation,
   neither shall they learn war anymore;
⁴ but they shall sit every man under his vine and under his fig tree,

and no one shall make them afraid,
for the mouth of Jehovah of armies[142] has spoken.

Experiencing what these two prophets have described can only bring us a sense of awe because all we knew in the physical world was conflict, war, bloodshed, and death.

However, when you believe there is an utopian reality as described by the prophets, it shouldn't be difficult to let go of this material world for the one God has prepared. This is why Jesus said, "I go to prepare a place for you. And if I go and prepare a place for you, I will come again and receive you to myself, so that where I am, you may be also." (John 14:2-3) Jesus is at work preparing an enteral home for the saints. Since Jesus is the builder of the eternal home, it is free from all the sinful contaminations of this physical world. There shall also be no decay for time is no more. It is senseless to covet this world's possessions when time only brings decay. This is why Jesus said, "For what does it profit a man to gain the whole world and forfeit his soul?" (Mark 8:36) The material is measurable; the soul is immeasurable. Charles G. Finney stated, "The worth of the world is a finite quantity, and can therefore be easily measured and estimated. But the worth of the soul is an ever-growing and in this sense a boundless, or infinite quantity, and can, therefore, never be estimated. The world is estimable; the soul is literally inestimable. No arithmetic can compute it; no finite mind grasp it. Indeed, God Himself must see that that which is an ever-growing quantity can never be compared with that the amount of which can be estimated and expressed in numbers.

---

[142] **Jehovah of armies**: (Heb. *jhvh tsaba*) literally means an army of soldiers, or military forces (Gen. 21:22; Deut. 20:9). It can also be used figuratively, "the sun and the moon and the stars, all the armies of heaven." (Deut. 4:19) In the plural form, it is also used of the Israelites forces as well. (Ex. 6:26; 7:4; Num. 33:1; Psa. 44:9) However, the "armies" in the expression "Jehovah of armies" is a reference to the angelic forces primarily, if not exclusively.

The value of the world, then, is as nothing against infinity. To gain the whole world would be to gain, after all, but little. And in fact, for a human being to possess the world, would be to him really no good at all; it would only load him with an ocean of cares, and anxieties, and perplexities, from which he could reap really no solid benefit. It would prove to him only what it did to Solomon; and Solomon, be it remembered, possessed as much of it as he knew what to do with. Like Solomon, he would find it vanity of vanities, and vexation of spirit."[143]

However, when a soul is saved who can really describe the ever increasing eternal bliss with God and Jesus Christ? It is hard to do; but imagine life with no pain, no sorrow, no crying, no sickness, no separation, no conflict, no war, no bloodshed, no politics, no racism, no classism, no poor, and no more death. Imagine being in a city that has twelve gates to it and the streets are paved with pure gold. Imagine living with no need for the sun and the moon. The glory of the Lord will be the eternal light. Can you imagine a crystal clear river with the tree of life on either side of it? The book of Revelation chapters 21-22 points out these realities, which are hard to imagine living in this fallen, marred, and sinful world. None of the realities of this material world that makes us weep and wail, fear and dread shall exist in the place Jesus Christ has prepared for His people.

What you must understand and have faith in is heaven is still under construction. People that you witness to about Christ and they give their hearts and minds to Christ, a mansion is added for their eternal habitation. In God's kingdom are many mansions. Mansions are usually houses that have many rooms. No one knows what this looks like in spiritual terms; but we can be assured that there is plenty of

---

[143] Cited from The Gospel Truth Ministries, 2000, Rev. Charles C. Finney, "Profit And Loss; Or The Worth Of The Soul," Pt.2, Published in The Oberlin Evangelist 1861, Index of Sermons.

space for each soul to enjoy comfort, joy, and contentment. The living arrangements in the mansions are not known. Maybe families will be joined together to live in each mansion never to be separated from one another again. Maybe each nation will occupy a mansion. We can only speculate the number of mansions and what the living arrangements shall be. But, whatever the living arrangements are, there won't be scrabbles and discord, for all of this is pass and gone forever. "The former things have passed away. (Revelation 21:4)

The love that you show and the work that you do for Jesus Christ, preparation is being made on your behalf to live eternally in the Kingdom of God. Once your soul leaves your body, you are ushered up by angels and personally welcomed by Jesus Christ to inherit God's Kingdom. "And so while your family tends to your funeral, you are beholding the face of Christ. Though the family weeps at your departure, you would not return to earth even if the choice were given to you. Having seen heaven, you will find that earth has lost all of its attraction. As Tony Evans says, 'Have a good time at my funeral, because I'm not going to be there.'"[144] You are now living in another realm of existence. The Scripture reminds us, "We shall be like him." (1 John 3:2) Whatever Jesus was able to do after his resurrection, we will be able to do also. Jesus was able to appear and disappear at will. He has a glorified body, and we too shall have a glorified body that functions just like Jesus.

Years ago, it was often said in the church, "One look in the Kingdom of God pays for it all." All of the experiences you have had on earth while serving God through Jesus Christ pales in comparison to what you shall live in heaven. The eternal joy and happiness are never ending. The fellowship with your family, friends, and loved ones who

---

[144] Erwin W. Lutzer, One Minute After You Die, Moody Publishers, 2015, 133-134.

made it to the Kingdom of God shall be an unending bond of love, laughter, and life. You will recognize your loved ones and the ones you never had a chance to meet on earth. "Think back to your background: your parents, brothers, sisters, family reunions. Of course, you will remember all of this and more in heaven. Do you actually think you might know less in heaven than you do on earth? Unthinkable! Once in heaven, we will soon get to meet a host of others, some known to us in this life or through the pages of church history, others nameless in this world but equally honored in the world to come. . . . In heaven there will be intuitive knowledge, for our minds will be redeemed from the limitations sin imposed upon them."[145] All we can say about heaven is it is a place of eternal reward. I don't want to miss living with God and Jesus Christ in this magnificent prepared place. As was said earlier, words cannot really describe the place Christ has prepared for the saints. Since, "Christ can do exceedingly abundantly above all that we can ask or think" while on earth, just think about what will be done for us while in heaven as an eternal reward. The following hymn by Rufus Henry Cornelius should encourage your heart to stay on the journey in light of your eternal reward.

> As I journey through the land, singing as I go,
> Pointing souls to Calvary—to the crimson flow,
> > Many arrows pierce my soul from without, within;
> > But my Lord leads me on, through Him I must win.
> > Oh, I want to see Him, look upon His face,
> > There to sing forever of His saving grace;
> > > On the streets of glory let me lift my voice,
> > > Cares all past, home at last, ever to rejoice.
> > When in service for my Lord dark may be the night,
> > > But I'll cling more close to Him, He will give me light;
> > > Satan's snares may vex my soul, turn my thoughts aside;

---

[145] Ibid., 88-89.

But my Lord goes ahead, leads whatever betide.
Oh, I want to see Him, look upon His face,
There to sing forever of His saving grace;
On the streets of glory let me lift my voice,
Cares all past, home at last, ever to rejoice.
When in valleys low I look toward the mountain height,
And behold my Savior there, leading in the fight,
With a tender hand outstretched toward the valley
low,
Guiding me, I can see, as I onward go.
Oh, I want to see Him, look upon His face,
There to sing forever of His saving grace;
On the streets of glory let me lift my voice,
Cares all past, home at last, ever to rejoice.
When before me billows rise from the mighty deep,
Then my Lord directs my bark; He doth safely keep,
And He leads me gently on through this world below;
He's a real Friend to me, oh, I love Him so.
Oh, I want to see Him, look upon His face,
There to sing forever of His saving grace;
On the streets of glory let me lift my voice,
Cares all past, home at last, ever to rejoice.[146]

---

[146] Refus H. Cornelius, "Oh, I Want to See Him," 1916.

CHAPTER TEN The Conclusion

2 Corinthians 13:5 Updated American Standard Version (UASV)

⁵ Keep testing yourselves to see if you are in the faith. Keep examining yourselves! Or do you not realize this about yourselves, that Jesus Christ is in you, unless indeed you fail to meet the test?

On this verse Edward D. Andrews writes,

> When was the last time that we truly took a good look at ourselves? How did we feel about what we saw? When we ponder over our personality, what are we actually projecting to others? Most of us are very complex people when it comes to our thoughts, feeling and beliefs, so it might be difficult to lock down what kind of personality that we have. As a man, are we faithful like Abraham one moment and then blown back and forth like doubting Thomas the next? As a female, are we submissive like Sarah when we are in public and then like domineering Jezebel in private? As a Christian, are we devoted and energetic for the truth on Christian meeting days and then loving the world like Demas[147] the other days out of the week? As a Christian, have we entirely taken off the old person with its practices and clothed ourselves with the new person? – Colossians 3:9-10; Ephesians 4:20-24.
>
> Some women are known to spend much time every morning, 'putting on their face,' as it is commonly

---

[147] A "fellow worker" with Paul at Rome (Col. 4:14; Philem. 24), who eventually, "in love with this present world," forsook the apostle and left for Thessalonica (2 Tim. 4:10). No other particulars are given concerning him. (ISBE, Volume 1, Page 918)

expressed. So much so, it has been commonly joked about, and men know not to interfere until the project is over. However, truth be told, men are very much concerned with how they look when going out into public. Thus, all of us are conscious of whether our hair is out of place, if we have a pimple or a cold sore, or if there is something about us that is unkempt, ruffled, scruffy, or messy. We want to look our best. What we may have not considered is, our personality, is always showing as well. The deeper question though is "are we putting on our personality to cover over before we go out in public while our real personality is on display in private?" Is what the public sees, who we really are? Does our real personality bring honor to God?

A man walking the roads of the countryside in a small European country comes to a fork in the road. He is uncertain as to which way he should go. Therefore, he asks several who are passing by for directions, but some told him to take the left fork, and others said to make the right. After receiving contradictory information, he simply did not know what to do, how was he to go on, without knowing for certain which path led to the destination. He was unable to move on until he knew what the right path was. Having doubts about our faith, our walk with God, his Word can influence us similarly. It can actually cause severe emotional turmoil as we go about our Christian life.

There was a similar situation on the first-century Corinthian congregation. Some known as "super-apostles" were actually taking the apostle Paul to task, as to Paul's walk with God, saying, "His letters are weighty and strong, but his bodily presence is weak, and his speech of no account." (2 Cor. 10:7-12; 11:5-6, ESV) Certainly, we can see how a Christian in that congregation could wonder if they were truly walking with God when the apostle Paul himself was being call into question.

Paul founded the Corinthian congregation in about 50 C.E.[148] on his second missionary journey. "When Silas and Timothy arrived from Macedonia, Paul was occupied with the word, testifying to the Jews that the Christ was Jesus. And the Lord said to Paul one night in a vision, 'Do not be afraid, but go on speaking and do not be silent, for I am with you, and no one will attack you to harm you, for I have many in this city who are my people.' And he stayed a year and six months, teaching the word of God among them." (Acts 18:5-11, ESV) The apostle Paul was deeply interested in the spiritual wellbeing of the brothers and sisters in Corinth. Moreover, the Corinthian Christians were interested in their spiritual welfare as well, so they wrote Paul for his counsel on certain matters. (1 Cor. 7:1-40) Therefore, Paul, under inspiration offered them inspired counsel in what would be his second letter to them.

"Keep testing yourselves to see if you are in the faith. Keep examining yourselves! Or do you not realize this about yourselves, that Jesus Christ is in you, unless indeed you fail to meet the test?" (2 Cor. 13:5) If these brothers in the days of having Paul found their congregation, who spent sixteen months under the guidance of the greatest, inspired Christian, needed to self-examine themselves, how much more should we need to do so, as we are 2,000-years removed. If these brothers followed this advice to examine themselves, it would have offered them direction on how to walk with God and let them know if they were on the right path.

Remember, Jesus warned, "Not everyone who says to me, 'Lord, Lord,' will enter the kingdom of heaven, but **the one who does** the will of my Father who is in

---

[148] B.C.E. means "before the Common Era," which is more accurate than B.C. ("before Christ"). C.E. denotes "Common Era," often called A.D., for *anno Domini*, meaning "in the year of our Lord."

heaven." (Matt 7:21, ESV) In other words, not every Christian was going to enter into the kingdom, even though they felt that they were walking with God. Jesus spoke of their mindset in the next verse, "On that day many will say to me, 'Lord, Lord, did we not prophesy in your name, and cast out demons in your name, and do many mighty works in your name?'" (Matt. 7:22, ESV) Yes, these ones, who felt that they were walking with God, on that day they were supposing that they were truly Christian, were in for a rude awakening. What is Jesus going to say to these ones, "And then will I declare to them, 'I never knew you; depart from me, you workers of lawlessness.'" (Matt. 7:23) What were and are these ones lacking?

Jesus said they were **not doing the will of the Father**, even though they believed they were. Notice that in 98 C.E., the apostle John, the last surviving apostle, in one of his letters offered that same warning too. He wrote, "The world is passing away, and its lusts; but the one who does the will of God remains forever." (1 John 2:17) Thus, we can see the wisdom of the apostle Paul's counsel to 'Keep testing ourselves to see if you are in the faith. Keep examining ourselves!' Thus, the next question is, what do we need to do to follow this advice? How does one test whether or not they are in the faith? In addition, what does it mean to 'keep examining ourselves after we have tested ourselves?

Keep Testing Yourselves

In a **test**, there is an examination of a person or an object to find something out, e.g. whether it is functioning properly or not. In this **test**, there must be a standard by which the person or object is measured. For example, the "normal" human body temperature is 98.6°F (37°C). Therefore, if we were testing our temperature, it would be measured against the normal body temperature. Anything above or below that would be considered high or low. Another example is the normal resting heart rate for adults, which ranges from 60 to 100 beats a minute. However, our test in this publication is to see if we are truly Christian. However, what we are looking for when we 'test ourselves, to see if we are in the faith,' **is not** the faith, that is the basic Bible doctrines. In our test, we are the subject. What we are testing is, if we are truly walking with God. If we are to test our walk as a Christian, we need to have a perfect standard. Our perfect standard by which to measure ourselves is,

Psalm 19:7-8 Updated American Standard Version (UASV)

⁷ The law of Jehovah is perfect,
    restoring the soul;
the testimony of Jehovah is sure,
    making wise the simple.
⁸ The precepts of Jehovah are right,
    rejoicing the heart;

Yes, the Word of God, the Bible is the standard by which we can measure our walk with God. On this, the author of Hebrews wrote, "For the word of God is living and active and sharper than any two-edged sword, and piercing as far as the division of soul and spirit, of both joints and marrow, and able to judge the thoughts and intentions of the heart." (Heb. 4:12) Thus, we must test our walk with God by examining our life course as outlined by Scripture, to find his favor, to be in an approved standing, to be declared righteous before him. Herein, each of the twenty chapters will have a text that they will be built around, a text that defines **what we should be** in the eyes of God. For example, several times Jesus says 'if we are doing _____, we are truly his disciples.' Well, the objective would be to discover what all is involved in doing _____.

Keep Examining Yourselves

The phrase keep *examining yourselves* is self-explanatory, but it involves a self-examination. We may have been a Christian for a number of years, but how many times have we had a spiritual checkup. Every six months we are to go in for a dental cleaning and unless there is a problem, we should get a health screening once a year. The problem with our spirituality is it is far more susceptible to injury than we are physically. The author of Hebrews warns us, "We must **pay much closer attention** to what we have heard, lest we **drift away** from it." (2:1) One chapter later, we are told, "**Take care**, brothers, lest there be in any of you *an evil, unbelieving heart*, leading you to **fall away** from the living God. But exhort one another every day, as long as it is called "today," that none of you may be **hardened by the deceitfulness of sin**." (3:12-13) This same author warns us about falling away (6:6), becoming sluggish (6:12), and growing weary or fainthearted (12:25).

Why would this be the case? If we are saved, why is it necessary that we keep examining ourselves? Why would we still be susceptible to bad behaviors to the point of drifting away, to the point of having an unbelieving heart, falling away, becoming sluggish, growing weary or fainthearted?

There are four reasons. **(1)** First and foremost, we have inherited sin, which means that we are missing the mark of perfection. **(2)** In addition, our environment can condition us into the bad thinking and behavior. **(3)** We have our human weaknesses, which include inborn tendencies that we naturally lean toward evil, leading us into bad behaviors. **(4)** Moreover, there is the world of Satan and his demons that caters to these human weaknesses, which also leads us down the path of bad thinking and behaviors. After our self-examination, what is needed if we are to overcome any bad thinking or behaviors and how are we to avoid developing them in the future? We will offer more on this in each chapter as well as two appendices at the end, but we offer this for now. It is paramount that we fully understand what all is involved in our human imperfection and never believe that we are so strong spiritually that we would never fall away, slow down, or becoming sluggish in our walk with God.

Obviously, this should be of the greatest concern to each one of us. We may be a person of good character, and believe that in any situation, we will make the right decisions. However, the moment that **innocent appearing situation** arises, we are plagued with the inner desire toward wrong. We need to address more than what our friends, or our workmates or our spouse may see. We need to look into our inner self, in the hopes of determining, who we really are, and what do we need to do to have a good heart (i.e., inner person).

As we know, we could not function with half a heart. However, we can function, albeit dysfunctional, with a heart that is divided. Yes, we have things outside of us that can contribute to bad thinking, which id left unchecked will lead to bad behavior, but we also have some things within. The apostle Paul bewailed about himself, "For I do not do the good I want, but the evil I do not want is what I keep on doing. Now if I do what I do not want, it is no longer I who do it, but sin that dwells within me." (Romans 7:19-20) This is because all of us are mentally bent toward the doing of wrong, instead of the doing of good. (Gen 6:5; 8:21; Rom 5:12; Eph. 4:20-24; Col 3:5-11) Jeremiah the prophet informs us of the condition of our heart (our inner person), "The heart is deceitful above all things, and desperately sick; who can understand it?" These factors contribute to our being more vulnerable to the worldly desires and the weak human flesh than we may have thought. One needs to understand just how bad human imperfection is before they can fully implement the right **Christian Living Skills.**

Returning to the book of Hebrews, we are told, "solid food belongs to the mature, to those who through practice have their discernment trained to distinguish between good and evil." (5:14) We will have evidence that we are one of the mature ones by training ourselves to distinguish between good and evil. We likely believe that we are already spiritually mature, which may very well be the case. Nevertheless, we are told by Paul to carry out this self-examination and to keep on examining ourselves, to remain that way, and even to improve upon what we currently have by way of maturity. Just as a man or woman in a marathon must continually train their muscles to surpass others in the sport, our discernment (perception) needs to be trained through regularly and rightly applying the Word of God. Throughout this publication, we will apply the inspired words of James, Jesus' half-brother.

James 1:22-25 Updated American Standard Version (UASV)

22 But be doers of the word, and not hearers only, deceiving yourselves. 23 For if anyone is a hearer of the word and not a doer, he is like a man who looks intently at his natural face[149] in a mirror.

24 for he looks at himself and goes away, and immediately forgets what sort of man he was. 25 But he that looks into the perfect law, the law of liberty, and abides by it, being no hearer who forgets but a doer of a

---

[149] Lit *the face of his birth*

work, he will be blessed in his doing.

When we are inundated in the Word of God, it serves as the voice of God, telling us the way in which to walk.[150]

Due to the secularization of our culture with its market-driven society, it is easy to think that today's practice of Christianity is about crowds, conventions, cash, and convenience. Many Christians have been duped by the methodology of gaining worldly status, material possessions, and becoming a religious celebrity. Christianity has become so peppered by the spices of this world that the Great Commission has been replaced by great consumerism of the church. It seems Christians are more into building buildings than building lives; more into Churchianity than Christianity; more into entertainment than enduring the ordeals of the cross. Too many Christians accommodate the culture while compromising Christ. The postmodern church is full of cultural Christians who allow the culture to dictate what is moral, right, and just, and not the Scriptures and the Holy Spirit. Due to a very skewed understanding of what Christianity is in today's culture, it is necessary to reemphasize what it means to be a true Christian, a follower of Jesus Christ.

As was stated earlier, much of what is labeled Christianity is not Christian at all. It is like a fig tree with nothing but leaves and no fruit. The leaves look good; they are very attractive, but the fig tree has no fruit. Jesus Christ is looking for fruit, not leaves. Much of practice of postmodern Christianity is leaves. Many of the programs, ministries, and conferences are spiritually unproductive because Christians are too intertwined with the world. Christians cannot expect to win the world for Christ while embracing at the same time the values and ethics they supposed to be trying to transform.

---

[150] Edward D. Andrews. *EVIDENCE THAT YOU ARE TRULY CHRISTIAN.* Cambridge: Christian Publishing House, 2015, pp. 2-7.

Jesus told followers, "No one can serve two masters; for either, he will hate the one and love the other, or he will be devoted to one and despise the other. You cannot serve God and wealth."[151] (Mathew 6:24)

Unless followers serve like, love like, and be willing to suffer like Jesus Christ, they should not call themselves Christians. True followers of Christ don't give sanction to an ungodly culture nor do they align themselves with social and political structures that arrange people into hierarchical categories of which oppression is underpinned and not undermined. Christians have a choice; they will be thermostats that set the temperature of society, or they will be thermometers that only register the temperature of society. They cannot be both lest they are become lukewarm a detriment to their souls. The enormous work and commitment to expanding God's Kingdom on earth must be done by the Word of God and the Holy Spirit. Any other way would be fruitless, which means followers of Christ must be faithful to his way and teachings for this is the only way to bring about the transformation of the nation. Too many Christians have given up on the transformation of the nation and of the world. The excuse is they point to Scriptures that say our present time is predicted, and since it is predicted there is nothing Christians can do to redeem it. Taking the position the Bible is fulfilling itself, many Christians sit back and believe that change will automatically blow in by the winds of inevitability. They do not understand that the change agents are themselves. As God was in Christ reconciling the world to Himself, Jesus was God's hands, feet, eyes, and tongue. Since followers are in Christ, they must be the hands, feet, eyes, and tongue of Christ as He was to God.

---

[151]   Gr., mamonai, dative, for Aram mamon (mammon); transliterated from the Aramaic; usually in a derogatory sense property, wealth, earthly goods (LU 16.9); personification Mammon, the Syrian god of riches, money (MT 6.24).

An anonymous person said, "A Christian is a mind through which Christ thinks; a heart through which Christ loves; a voice through which Christ speaks; a hand through which Christ helps."

The journey with Christ is by no means easy. It is an arduous and tiring journey which tests people's souls. Any teachings and writings that say to the contrary about how the journey with Jesus is pleasant and non-threatening is untrue. A great disservice is done when people try to sanitize and deodorize the journey with Jesus. There is nothing pleasant about bearing a cross, and for this reason, it is my sincere hope and prayer that this book has stunned readers in such a way that they do some serious reflecting and repenting if they have discovered they are not really following Christ. It is so easy to follow an idea and not the idealist. The journey with Jesus Christ is a lifelong commitment; and Christians must stop and examine themselves to see if they are really doing their Master's will, and if they are doing His will while undergoing the distresses of the cross, here are comforting words of the Savior,

Revelation 3:8-12 English Standard Version (ESV)

8 "'I know your works. Behold, I have set before you an open door, which no one is able to shut. I know that you have but little power, and yet you have kept my word and have not denied my name. 9 Behold, I will make those of the synagogue of Satan who say that they are Jews and are not, but lie—behold, I will make them come and bow down before your feet, and they will learn that I have loved you. 10 Because you have kept my word about patient endurance, I will keep you from the hour of trial that is coming on the whole world, to try those who dwell on the earth. 11 I am coming soon. Hold fast what you have, so that no one may seize your crown. 12 The one who conquers, I will make him a pillar in the temple of my God. Never shall he go out of it, and I will write on him the name of my God,

and the name of the city of my God, the new Jerusalem, which comes down from my God out of heaven, and my own new name.

In conclusion, continue on the journey because we have a Christ too precious to hide, a journey too thrilling to miss, and a Kingdom too great to inherit to stop now. "Press on toward the goal of for the prize of the upward call of God in Christ Jesus."

Bibliography

Anyabwile, Thabiti M., The Faithful Preacher, Crossway Books, 2007.

Benton, Don, The Cost of Being Christian, C.SS. Publishing Company, 1989.

Borthwich, Paul, Six Dangerous Questions to Transform Your View of the World, InterVarity Press, 1996.

Brill, Earl H., The Christian Moral Vision, The Seaburg Press, 1979.

Bonhoeffer, Dietrich, The Cost of Discipleship, Collier Books, 1963.

_____, Creation And Fall, Temptation Two Biblical Studies, Simon & Schuster Publisher, 1959.

Carter, Mack King, Interpreting the Will of God, Principle for Unlocking the Mystery, Judson Press, 2002.

Crabtree, T.T., The Pastor's Annual An Idea and Resource Book, Zondervan Publishing House, 1995.

Crockett, Kent, Pastor Abusers When Sheep Attack Their Shepherd, Whole Armor Press, 2012.

Dixon, Larry, When Temptation Strikes, CLC Publications, 2008.

Douglass, Frederick, Life & Times of Frederick Douglass, MacMillan Publishing Company, 1962.

Evans, Tony, No More Excuses Be the Man God Made You to Be, Crossway Books, 1996.

_____, Speaks Out On Spiritual Warfare, Moody Press, 2000.

Evans, Colleen Townsend, The Vine Life, Chosen Books Publishing Company, 1980.

Fosdick, Harry Emerson, Answers to Real Problems: Harry Emerson Fosdick Speaks to Our Time, Wipf & Stock Publishers, 2008.

Francis, James Allan, The Real Jesus and Other Sermons, Judson Press, 1926.

Galli, Mark & Olsen, Ted, 131 Christians Everyone Should Know, Broadman & Holman Publishers, 2000.

Hammarberg, Melvin A., "To Dream the Impossible Dream," Augsburg Sermons Series C, Augsburg Publishing House, 1973.

Howard, Thurman, Deep Is the Hunger, Friends United Press, 1951.

_____, Jesus and the Disinherited, Friends United Press, 1981.

Idle, Kyle, Not A Fan Becoming A Completely Committed Follower of Jesus, Zondervan, 2011.

Khan, Hazrat Inayat, The Inner Life, Shambhala Publications, 1997.

Kierkegaard, Soren, Training In Christianity, Princeton University Press, 1972.

King Jr., Martin Luther, Strength To Love, Fortress Press, 1963.

Kuehn, Krystal, "Betrayal: When Someone You Love Betrays You," SelfGrowth.com, 2010.

Luther, Erwin W., When A Nation Forgets God, Moody Publishers, 2010.

_____, One Minute After You Die, Moody Publisher, 2015.

_____, Your Eternal Reward, Triumph And Tears at the Judgment Seat of Christ, Moody Publishers, 2015.

MacArthur, John, The Gospel According to Jesus: What Is Authentic Faith?, Zondervan, 2008.

Moore, Russell D., Tempted And Tried: Temptation and the Triumph of Christ, Crossway Publisher, 2011.

Niebuhr, Richard H., Christ and Culture, Harper & Row, 1951.

Nouwen, Henri J. M., The Wounded Healer, Image Book, 1979.

O'Murchu, Diarmaid, Christianity's Dangerous Memory, A Rediscovery of the Revolutionary Jesus, Crossroad Publishing Company, 2011.

Owens, John, Overcoming Sin & Temptation, Crossway Books, 2006.

Piper, John, Mathis, David, Think It Not Strange Navigating Trials In the New America, Published by Desiring God, 2016.

Platt, David, What Did Jesus Really Mean When He Said Follow Me, Tyndale House Publisher, 2013.

_____, Counter Culture: A Compassionate Call to Counter Culture in a World of Poverty, Same-Sex Marriage, Racism, Sex Slavery, Immigration, Abortion, Persecution, Orphans and Pornography, Tyndale House Publishers, 2015.

Prochnow, Herbert V., The Speaker's Book of Illustrations, Baker Book House, 1960.

Puritan, Edward Earle, The Triumph of the Man Who Acts, Efficiency Publishing Company, 1916.

Ray, Sandy F., Journey Through A Jungle, Broadman Press, 1979.

Schlessinger, Dr. Laura, Surviving A Shark Attack On Land: Overcoming Betrayal and Dealing With Revenge, Harper Collins, 2011.

Tozer, A. W., Man the Dwelling Place of God, Fig Publisher, 2012.

Washington, James Melvin, Martin Luther King, Jr., A Testament of Hope, The Essential Writings of Martin Luther King, Jr., Harper & Row Publishers, 1986.

Wiberforce, William, Real Christianity, Regal Books, 2006.

Winch, Guy, Emotional First Aid, Hudson Street Press, 2013.

Wolbrecht, Walter F., "The Temptations of Christ, the Church, and the Christian," Augsburg Sermon Series C, Augsburg Publishing House, 1973.

Yow, Jesse, Standing Firm A Christian Response to Hostility and Persecution, Concordia Publishing House, 2015.

Hymns cited:

GIA Publications

African American Heritage Hymnal

The United Methodist Hymnal

Hymnology.com